PEN

BY DAVID MARSHALL GRANT

★

DRAMATISTS
PLAY SERVICE
INC.

★

To my parents and Wendy and Tom with love.
And for K.C., who has made everything possible.

PEN was produced by Playwrights Horizons (Tim Sanford, Artistic Director; Leslie Marcus, Managing Director; William Russo, General Manager) in New York City, opening on April 2, 2006. It was directed by Will Frears; the set design was by Robin Vest; the costume design was by Jenny Mannis; the lighting design was by Mathew Richards; the sound design was by Obadiah Eaves; and the stage manager was Carmen I. Abrazado. The cast was as follows:

HELEN BAYER .... J. Smith-Cameron
MATT BAYER .... Dan McCabe
JERRY BAYER .... Reed Birney

PEN was presented in a reading at New York Stage and Film Company (Mark Lyn-Baker, Max Mayer, Leslie Urdang, Producing Directors; Elizabeth Timperman, Managing Producer) at Vassar College in Poughkeepsie, New York, in July 2004. It was directed by Will Frears. The cast was as follows:

HELEN BAYER .... Marcia Gay Harden
MATT BAYER .... Kieran Culkin
JERRY BAYER .... Dennis Boutsikaris

CHARACTERS

HELEN BAYER, Matt's mother, early forties

MATT BAYER, seventeen

JERRY BAYER, Matt's father, forties

PLACE

New York City.

TIME

October – December 1969.

"From each according to his abilities,
to each according to his needs."

— *Karl Marx*

PEN

ACT ONE

Scene 1

October 1969. Lights up on a living room. The set should look like it floats in space. The furniture is simple and sparse. Helen Bayer, early forties, sits in a wheelchair. She wears plain stretch pants under a fall coat. She's got a hair-do that requires a visit to the hairdresser. Matt Bayer, seventeen, her son, wears a tie and a rumpled corduroy jacket. They have both just come in from outside.

HELEN. Well, that was an unmitigated disaster.

MATT. Will you stop it, Mom, it went fine.

HELEN. I can't imagine what kind of impression we made. Why didn't you tell me I lost an earring? I must have looked like a complete idiot. Or a pirate.

MATT. She was just some sophomore giving a tour.

HELEN. Well, she has some influence on the admissions process or she wouldn't be giving it.

MATT. She was wearing braces. I wouldn't worry about it.

HELEN. Well, that's where you're wrong. College is very serious business. There's nothing you shouldn't worry about. I can't believe your father, strolling in thirty minutes late.

MATT. I thought he hit if off really well with her.

HELEN. Of course he did. She was eighteen. What in God's name were they talking about?

MATT. Stereos. Her parents just got her one.

HELEN. What kind of kid needs a stereo?

MATT. Maybe someone who wants to play records.

HELEN. What's wrong with a transistor radio?

MATT. It doesn't play records.

HELEN. Well, she seemed like an idiot.

MATT. She wasn't an idiot. She was very nice.

HELEN. Of course, I'm wearing only one earring. What do I know?

MATT. We'll find the other one.

HELEN. No, it's lost. It's dead to me now. Dead. If only I could manage a proper pair of pierced earrings. This is what happens when you're forced to wear clip-ons. *(Matt starts to help her off with her coat.)* Ouch. Don't bend my arm. I assume he's alright, your father. He never talks to me.

MATT. He's fine.

HELEN. Hang that up properly. I have to wear it to the Krugman's Sukkoth party. It's the only decent thing I own. I may just leave it on the whole night.

MATT. I thought you were going shopping tomorrow.

HELEN. It's too last minute. I'll never find anything. And it's October. Everything's between seasons. Where's my purse?

MATT. *(Handing it to her.)* Here.

HELEN. Your father didn't mention "her," did he?

MATT. Not to me.

HELEN. Well, maybe he's on to someone else.

MATT. It's not like he just met her.

HELEN. There's no shortage of young women, you know.

MATT. She's thirty-two.

HELEN. Now.

MATT. Mom, she's old, okay.

HELEN. I don't know what's worse. She's thirty-two or you think that's old.

MATT. Do you want help getting on the couch? I'm going to the movies.

HELEN. You're not taking the car. It's been used enough today.

MATT. We drove five exits. Maximum.

HELEN. There was an op-ed piece about smog today.

MATT. You're going shopping with Mrs. Lyons tomorrow.

HELEN. That's different. I have to go to this Sukkoth party. Did you send her a note yet?

MATT. I will.

HELEN. You have to send her a note.

MATT. I will.

HELEN. You can't imagine what she's going through.

MATT. I know.

HELEN. No, you don't. That poor family. It's never been easy. They had big problems. Both those kids had big problems.

MATT. Ruth is fine. She goes to Brown.

HELEN. Well, she wanted to go to Yale.

MATT. I wouldn't call that a huge problem.

HELEN. Not for you. You couldn't get into either. Help me onto the couch.

MATT. Get on the couch yourself.

HELEN. I've been out all day. I'm tired.

MATT. Alright. Come on.

HELEN. Take the legs off first.

MATT. *(Taking the legs off.)* I know!

HELEN. You really have to send them a note.

MATT. I will.

HELEN. There was a whole article in *The Times*. Drug use is skyrocketing in suburbia. It's a catastrophe.

MATT. Andy Lyons killed himself. It had nothing to do with drugs.

HELEN. Well, that's where you're wrong. Drugs drove him to it.

MATT. Maybe he would have killed himself years ago and it was only drugs that were keeping him happy for a while. Have you ever thought of that?

HELEN. Not for an instant. You know, if that is your assessment of Andy Lyons' death, that the only thing keeping him alive was LSD, maybe you're going to the wrong psychiatrist.

MATT. He blames you for everything, you know. I can't believe you pay him.

HELEN. I don't pay him. Your father does. If I paid him, he'd blame your father. They know where their bread is buttered.

MATT. He blames him, too.

HELEN. How do you contribute to your problems?

MATT. He's not judgmental about me.

HELEN. That's interesting, since you were the one arrested.

MATT. For shoplifting.

HELEN. Stealing is stealing. Maybe he should judge a little.

MATT. You know what, I'm not supposed to talk to you about this. You're the last person I'm supposed to talk about it to.

HELEN. Why don't you just leave then? Clearly I make you miserable.

MATT. I'm trying to. You won't let me take the car.

HELEN. And by the way, I'm not at all sure Pat Lyons will even want to take me shopping tomorrow. Not that you care.

MATT. I don't care. You're right. I don't care about anyone but me.

HELEN. Just write her a note. It's a complete nightmare. Your worst.

MATT. I promise I'll write her a note.

HELEN. Don't bother. There's nothing you can say. Apparently, she was at Waldbaums and someone came up and said their prayers were with her. Why someone would say such a thing at a time like that, I'll never know.

MATT. I think they were trying to help.

HELEN. Well, there is no solace. You live with that for the rest of your life, the death of a child. Just help me on the couch. I'm tired.

MATT. *(Standing next to her.)* Are you ready?

HELEN. *(Looking at the coffee table.)* Where's my pen?

MATT. Come on.

HELEN. What did you do with my pen?

MATT. I didn't touch your pen.

HELEN. It's not here. It's always right next to the newspaper.

MATT. It's somewhere.

HELEN. Where?

MATT. I don't know.

HELEN. You must have taken it. Pens don't vanish into thin air.

MATT. I didn't take your pen, Mom. It's here somewhere. Can we just get you on the couch.

HELEN. I want to finish the crossword puzzle.

MATT. *(Picking up another pen.)* Here. This seems like a very nice pen.

HELEN. That's useless. I'm talking about the red one, for Christ's sake. It's got to be here somewhere.

MATT. I'll look later, okay. The movie starts in fifteen minutes.

HELEN. Who are you going with?

MATT. No one.

HELEN. You can't go see a movie by yourself.

MATT. Why not?

HELEN. Because it's embarrassing. People will think you're desperate.

MATT. I am.

HELEN. Well, you need to make friends. I don't understand why you don't have any friends. What happened to that Chapman boy?

MATT. Ian? I don't know. That was sixth grade.

HELEN. You should have invited him over here.

MATT. You hated him. His parents voted for Goldwater.

HELEN. I never took that out on Ian. Honestly. You have the worst memory.

MATT. How can I remember anything? You hide all the pictures.

HELEN. I didn't hide them. I organized them.

MATT. They're in the attic.

HELEN. Mrs. Green put them in albums. They're neatly stacked behind the baby clothes.

MATT. You saved my baby clothes?

HELEN. What do you think I did, burn them? I saved all your finger paintings, too, and they were awful.

MATT. Can I please go to the movies?

HELEN. No. We haven't had dinner. And you still haven't finished your application. You're applying early decision. That means you have to do it early. We didn't go to Stony Brook today for a lark.

MATT. I don't know what to write about.

HELEN. Yes, you do. We decided you were going to write about the scourge of injustice.

MATT. I don't even know what the scourge of injustice is.

HELEN. Well, let me tell you. The world is in trouble. Big trouble. It's astonishing how quickly we look the other way. Your father and I went with the Gardeners and the Krugmans and another couple on a driving holiday through Europe, and the other couple, who will remain nameless, they wanted to go to Germany. Can you imagine such a thing? Pigs would fly before Ken Gardener stepped foot in Germany again.

MATT. I know. He won't even buy a Volkswagon.

HELEN. That's goddamn right. Some things you don't forget. Some things you don't trivialize.

MATT. I just want to see a movie. I promise I won't trivialize the holocaust.

HELEN. Just write your essay. I don't understand what happened to that pen. It was sitting right here. Look under the couch.

MATT. Why can't you just use another one?

HELEN. Because it's the only one that works. *(Matt bends down and looks under the couch for the pen.)* Matt, you didn't take it, did you?

MATT. No.

HELEN. Are you sure, because …

MATT. I can't believe you're accusing me.

HELEN. Okay. Forget it.

MATT. I didn't take your precious pen!

HELEN. Alright, you lost it.

MATT. I didn't lose it either!

HELEN. The hell with it. You'll never find it. It's gone forever now. Just forget it. Get up.

MATT. Can I please just look now? I'm on my hands and knees.

HELEN. Don't bother. Mrs. Green just vacuumed down there. She would have noticed.

MATT. You want to know what Doctor Klein says? You're a pessimist. You make everything seem impossible.

HELEN. Well, some things are. *(Matt gets up, holding something.)*

MATT. Here.

HELEN. Did you find it?

MATT. It's your other earring.

HELEN. Let me see.

MATT. Back from the dead. You're lucky Mrs. Green didn't suck it up.

HELEN. I can't believe it.

MATT. I know. Your favorite earring. Brought back to life.

HELEN. Okay, I get it. Ha, ha. Thank you, but you were looking for my pen.

MATT. At least you have something to wear to the Krugman's Sukkoth party.

HELEN. If I go. If I can get there.

MATT. You're going. The Gardeners are taking you. Unless it's in Germany. Is the party in Germany?

HELEN. Ha, ha. You're so funny. What you don't know is Ken Gardener's getting too fat to pull me up stairs. And the Krugmans have a lot of stairs. God forbid there should be a ramp somewhere in this country.

MATT. Someone will take you.

HELEN. I wouldn't care except they make such a big deal of this party. Everything they do has to be "perfect." She cooks Brussel sprouts with Vermont maple syrup. We used to throw an election night party that rivaled hers. Oh, well, those days are dead and gone.

MATT. *I'll* take you to the Krugmans, alright? Mom, this movie starts in five minutes.

HELEN. Go to your room. See if my pen's in there.

MATT. I don't have your pen!

HELEN. This is a nightmare.

MATT. It's just a pen.

HELEN. It's not just a pen! I need that pen! I write lying down. It's the only one that doesn't dry up because of the angle. I'm constantly having to shake the other goddamn pens in order to bring the ink back down.

MATT. Who makes it? Maybe you can buy another one.

HELEN. The company's out of business. I called the store.

MATT. I'm sure they have something like it.

HELEN. Well, that's where you're wrong. They don't. It was designed for the moon. It's a zero gravity pen and the only place I can find it now would be NASA. I'll just have to shake pens for the rest of my goddamn life. Would you please get me on the couch.

MATT. I've been ready for ten minutes. *(Standing next to Helen.)*

HELEN. Don't rush me. Ouch. Lock the chair *(She takes hold of his arm.)*

MATT. I am. One, two ...

HELEN. Stand closer.

MATT. I am. One, two, three ... *(With Matt's help, Helen stands, pivots and sits down on the couch. Matt pulls the wheelchair aside.)*

HELEN. Put the pillow with the legs.

MATT. I know.

HELEN. Push the coffee table back.

MATT. I will.

HELEN. Put some Stouffer's in the oven.

MATT. I don't have time. I'll make you a sandwich.

HELEN. I don't want a sandwich. I want Stouffer's.

MATT. Aren't you sick of Stouffer's? You know, some families actually eat food that isn't frozen. And they have things besides stale Oreos for dessert.

HELEN. I like them when they're stale. They're chewy. Goddamn it, where's the remote control?

MATT. Right here. *(Matt gets it for her.)*

HELEN. Don't leave the remote control where I can't reach it.

MATT. Yeah, yeah, yeah.

HELEN. I mean it! It's not funny. Push the coffee table back. *(Matt goes into the kitchen.)* When you're crippled, you can have your own remote control. *(She aims the remote control. Eventually, the TV comes on ... the seven o'clock news on CBS. A story about Christmas in Vietnam.)*

MATT. *(Returning.)* Do you want chicken salad or center cut tongue

HELEN. You're not going to a movie.

15

MATT. Yes, I am.

HELEN. Quiet. The news is on.

MATT. I can't believe this. *(On TV Bob Hope is entertaining the troops in Saigon.)*

HELEN. I hate this man. He's evil.

MATT. Bob Hope?

HELEN. Well, he hasn't been funny in years.

MATT. I think he's hilarious. *(Matt sits in the wheelchair and laughs at one of the jokes.)*

HELEN. I can't watch this. It's wrong.

MATT. It's hilarious.

HELEN. It's not hilarious. It's wrong. Half those kids are going to be killed tomorrow and he's telling jokes.

MATT. He's a comedian.

HELEN. The Smothers Brothers are comedians. He's a company man. *(She changes the station.)*

MATT. Leave it. You don't have to be a hawk to like Bob Hope. *(Channel 5 has a commercial for Fresca. Matt's rolling around on the wheelchair, even doing wheelies.)* Oh, this is a good one. *(Helen lowers the volume.)* Turn it up!

HELEN. It's a commercial.

MATT. I like commercials.

HELEN. Stop staying that. They're the lowest of the low.

MATT. I like commercials, okay. I like them. *(The news has returned. Nixon is featured. She turns the volume back up.)*

HELEN. Nixon is so depressing, I don't know where to begin.

MATT. I love commercials. I'm going to make commercials when I grow up.

HELEN. He's an absolute disgrace.

MATT. I'm going to make commercials for Nixon and Agnew.

HELEN. Don't even say that. I can't listen to this. *(Referring to the wheelies.)* Stop playing with the chair!

MATT. Why?

HELEN. I won't be able to reach it.

MATT. Oh, boy, I guess I'll have to put it back when I'm finished. What a challenge.

HELEN. Stop being sarcastic. You're going to break the goddamn chair. Stop it! *(Matt stops. He gets off the chair and with great exaggeration and precision puts it back exactly where he found it.)*

MATT. There. Is that the *perfect* position?

HELEN. Lock it.

MATT. Let me check to see if there's any damage.

HELEN. Don't make fun of me. I need to be able to reach the chair. *(Matt starts to walk away.)* Where are you going?

MATT. I'M NOT GOING ANYWHERE.

HELEN. Stop shouting.

MATT. HOW CAN I GO ANYWHERE? YOU NEVER LET ME.

HELEN. Please, I have no control over you. I can't even get you to write a college application. I thought you wanted to get away from here.

MATT. I'll be eleven minutes down the LIE. Whoopee. And why do I have to apply early decision? There are other colleges in the world besides Stony Brook.

HELEN. It's a state school. Other colleges cost money.

MATT. Well, maybe Dad could pay. That's what he said.

HELEN. Excuse me?

MATT. Dad. He just got some money.

HELEN. From whom?

MATT. He got an advance. He sold another book. He said he could pay for college.

HELEN. Nonsense.

MATT. He's buying me a car.

HELEN. He's what?

MATT. He's buying me a car for Christmas. He told me at Andy Lyons' memorial service.

HELEN. That's preposterous. You don't need a car.

MATT. I could use one tonight.

HELEN. There are people who don't have food in this world and he's buying you a car? Fine. If that's the way he wants to look at the world. I certainly can't compete with that. Nor would I ever want to.

MATT. What's wrong with having enough money to buy me a car?

HELEN. This is what you and your father talked about at a funeral? A car? The body wasn't even cold yet and you two were car shopping?

MATT. He just told me and I listened.

HELEN. There's a smog crisis in this country.

MATT. Tell *him,* okay! It wasn't my idea to get me a car.

HELEN. What other colleges is he suggesting you apply to?

MATT. You don't know anything. You think you do, but you don't.

HELEN. He wants you to go to USC, doesn't he?

MATT. *(Heading for his coat.)* I'm going to see the last half hour of this movie.

HELEN. You can't count on his money, Matt. His only previously published book sold ten copies. Anyway, you couldn't possibly get in. Your SAT scores hardly —

MATT. I got a 690.

HELEN. Verbal. So, you know what loquacious means. Your math was atrocious.

MATT. You just don't want me to leave. You probably think I'm going to live here and commute to college.

HELEN. Well, you'll have a car.

MATT. It's a sports car, by the way. A German sports car. It sits so low, you'll never be able to get in it.

HELEN. I see. Well, the joke's on me. You know what, go to USC. See if I care. Watch football for the rest of your life. *(Silence.)*

MATT. Don't get all upset. I'm not going to California.

HELEN. I must seem pathetic to you. Last Christmas I was reduced to buying you two flannel shirts from the L.L. Bean catalogue. It's a far cry from German precision engineering, I know.

MATT. It's not a competition.

HELEN. Just go see your movie.

MATT. You know, Mom ... I don't even care about the car. I'm not even into cars. *(Beat.)* I'll put some Stouffer's in for dinner. *(Matt goes into the kitchen.)*

HELEN. Matt, we live in very dangerous times. There are people who simply don't care. And they are running this country. It's a fiasco. They care only about themselves. Now, if your father wants to buy you a sports car, that's his business, I'm just saying there are values more important than that. People are dying every day in a senseless war. Black people in this country are denied basic human rights. That's the scourge of injustice. To know that you care about these things is very important.

MATT. *(Reentering.)* There's only Turkey Tetrazzini left. I put them in.

HELEN. My legs are twitching now. Damn it.

MATT. Why do they shake?

HELEN. I don't know. They're angry. *(Matt gets up and goes to the end of the couch. He begins to press Helen's feet forward in a stretch.)*

MATT. Do you think you're getting worse?

HELEN. I'm not getting any better.

MATT. Have the doctors figured out anything?

HELEN. What are they going to figure out? It's incurable. *(Off his massage.)* That feels so good. Thank you. *(Beat.)* You're so sweet. Do you know that? Has anyone ever told you how sweet you are?

Look at you. You're so handsome. I'm so glad I made you get a haircut. You have ears again. I'm going to have to give you an earmuff for Christmas.

MATT. What do you want for Christmas?

HELEN. Just write your application to Stony Brook.

MATT. Come on. What do you want?

HELEN. I don't want anything. That's the trick. If you don't want anything, you're never disappointed.

MATT. Come on. What do you want?

HELEN. *(Singing.)* "All I want for Christmas is my two front teeth." When you were little I used to sing that to you.

MATT. I needed my two front teeth then.

HELEN. "All I want for Christmas is my two front teeth." Of course, you got your two front teeth. I could have used a little more help than that.

MATT. Remember when I was in third grade? I offered to wrap up my legs and give them to you?

HELEN. I should have let you. Maybe I will next time.

MATT. Sorry, it was a one time offer. *(Matt gets up.)*

HELEN. Where are you going?

MATT. To get an Aspirin. I have a headache.

HELEN. Give me the car keys. And, put some peas on, while you're up. We've got to have vegetables. *(Matt walks to the kitchen. Something catches his eye under a chair. He leans over to get a better look.)* What is it?

MATT. Nothing. I thought I saw your pen. *(Careful not to be seen, he picks up her pen and continues into the kitchen. Fade to black.)*

Scene 2

Two months later. Mid-December. A nice restaurant. Jerry Bayer, 40s, sits with Matt. There's a wrapped present on the table. They're on the salad course. Jerry's filling out a form and nursing a drink.

JERRY. What's your social security number?

MATT. O45-67-9872

JERRY. The Germans make the best cars, you know. Precision engineering.

MATT. You should hear Mom on the subject. It's like she's waiting for the arrival of a war criminal.

JERRY. She has a hard time letting go of things. I'm putting down you're parking the car in Long Island. We'll change that when we know what's going on. Although maybe we can just keep it like that. Car insurance is always cheaper in the suburbs.

MATT. I don't think she'll let me do that if I'm not living there.

JERRY. You know, if this is going to become a huge issue, I can just cancel it. The last thing I need —

MATT. No, don't. I want it.

JERRY. I haven't even driven it off the lot yet, so —

MATT. No. I want it. I do.

JERRY. I don't understand why you had to tell her.

MATT. It just came out.

JERRY. Loose lips sink ships, Matt.

MATT. She was going to find out anyway.

JERRY. But we lost our biggest advantage. Timing. Right? When and how she found out.

MATT. I didn't mean to. I'm sorry. I can handle it.

JERRY. You're right. It probably wouldn't have made any difference when you told her. *(Going back to the form.)* You deserve this. I'm proud of you. You really worked hard on this college thing. You waited till the very last minute, but I think you wrote a hell of an essay. To advance the value of advertising on our culture ... I think you scored a touch down.

MATT. Well, a field goal.

JERRY. I don't know what happened to you, but you got motivated.

MATT. I wrote another one called "The Scourge of Injustice."

JERRY. "The Scourge of Injustice"? Where did you come up with that?

MATT. Where do you think?

JERRY. Let me have three guesses —

MATT. JERRY. *(Sharing a laugh.)* And the first two don't count.

MATT. You don't think I should have mentioned the shoplifting stuff, right?

JERRY. No. We did the right thing. The question was about felonies.

MATT. What if they check?

JERRY. Shoplifting is nothing. You just need to think positively right now.

MATT. That's what I'm doing. I am.

JERRY. Good. *(Folding up the forms.)* I'll get this to Prudential in the morning. When you get the proof of insurance card, keep it in the car. Oh, man, I wish I had the time to drive cross-country. I'm so jealous. Here. I think it's running out of ink. *(Jerry hands Matt the pen.)*

MATT. That's okay. She has refills.

JERRY. I can't believe she let you take it. You know, she claims NASA makes them.

MATT. She lost it. I found it on the floor.

JERRY. When?

MATT. A couple of months ago.

JERRY. What?

MATT. A couple of months ago.

JERRY. Are you trying to get us both killed? If she knew we had this pen —

MATT. What?

JERRY. You can't just steal her pen.

MATT. I didn't, I found it.

JERRY. Well, give it back.

MATT. OK. *(Beat.)* Dr. Klein thinks I should keep it.

JERRY. He does? Really? Well, he would, he's a Freudian. You know, I'm not going to get involved in this. This is between you and your mother.

MATT. Why don't you open your present now?

JERRY. Alright, fine. Fine. *(Picking up the present.)* I wonder what it is. *(Unwrapping the gift.)* I never even saw that pen today, do you understand?

MATT. I understand.

JERRY. *(Holding an album.)* Oh, wow. Lester Young. This is great. *Live at the Royal Roost.* Thanks. This is very groovy.

MATT. They said it was rare.

JERRY. This is a classic, Matt.

MATT. Merry Christmas.

JERRY. He's a genius. This one's amazing.

MATT. You have it already?

JERRY. I have all of Lester Young.

MATT. They said this one was really rare.

JERRY. Nothing's too rare for me.

MATT. I'm sorry. I'll get you something else.

JERRY. Don't bother. I'll exchange it.

MATT. I don't think you can return it. It was on sale.

JERRY. I'll exchange it. There's always something I want. Where did you get it?

MATT. At a record store.

JERRY. Which one?

MATT. Some record store in the city.

JERRY. Where did you go? Near me? Greenwich Village? Rhino Records? Just give me the receipt, I'll exchange it.

MATT. I didn't steal it.

JERRY. I didn't say you did.

MATT. Yes, you did!

JERRY. *Shss.* No, I didn't, Matt. *(Beat.)* I'll keep it, okay. Mine's probably scratched. I don't think you stole it. *(Beat.)* How's Doctor Klein going?

MATT. I'm not supposed to talk about it.

JERRY. I understand. But you're feeling better? I know this has been a hard time for you — your parents splitting up and all. But you really seem like you're getting a handle on things. *(Beat.)* You are, right? *(Beat.)* Did you tell Klein about your essay? *(Beat.)* You know, when I was a kid I was caught shoplifting, too. I had two packets of baseball cards in my pocket and some chocolate cigarettes.

MATT. I know, you told me.

JERRY. I never had that many friends either. Look, I'm just glad you're feeling good. You're not doing any drugs, are you? That's what we call a rhetorical question. You should know what rhetorical means — 690 on your SAT's

MATT. Verbal. My math sucked.

JERRY. But you're not ...

MATT. No. And, by the way, "rhetorical" means you know the answer is "yes."

JERRY. I stand corrected. I never told your mother about that night I came home —

MATT. Dad.

JERRY. Whatever you were on, I got to admit it was pretty funny watching you try to eat macaronis. They kept dropping off the fork. You started sliding each individual macaroni onto each of the little fork spears.

MATT. Dad.

JERRY. Look, I understand. Kids experiment. Forget it. All this stuff is between you and Klein. I would never pry. Anyway ... This is fun tonight, right? Hey, you want to go watch the ball drop on New Year's Eve? I'm going to be all alone. Sally's got to be in LA. Come on, it'd be good for us to talk some more.

MATT. About what?

JERRY. I don't know. Stuff.

MATT. There's something I need to …

JERRY. What?

MATT. I told Mom about your new book.

JERRY. You did? What did she say?

MATT. She said the other one didn't sell very well.

JERRY. She will never understand.

MATT. How are you going to pay for college if —

JERRY. That was a trade book. It sold just fine.

MATT. Well, what's this one?

JERRY. Well, let me tell you. Do you know this book, *I'm OK — You're OK*? It tries to confront the individual with the fact that he or she is largely responsible for what happens in their life. Both good and bad. My book's a little more expansive but it has a similar point. Basically I'm asking why we can't truly own our own lives.

MATT. I don't know.

JERRY. Well, we can. That's the thing. And I want to tell you, the publishers are very excited about it. Dreams can come true. They're putting that on the dust jacket. I'm sure your mother will find the whole thing unbearably trite, but …

MATT. Well, her dreams didn't come true.

JERRY. I understand that, Matt, but we still have to try. We have to try and be happy. You don't have to be responsible for her, Matt. Do you understand that? Look at you. You've got your whole life ahead of you. You're in the driver's seat now. Literally. Man, you must be sitting on pins and needles. When do you find out?

MATT. Soon.

JERRY. USC is such a great school. I loved it. And really, most of the "campus problems" you hear about, that's up north. Berkeley. USC is more traditional.

MATT. She thinks it's a party school, you know.

JERRY. Well, she's wrong.

MATT. She said people major in football.

JERRY. That's ridiculous. She just hates the Trojans because they win every year. She resents anyone who wins. "The scourge of injustice." Sometimes I think the only injustice she sees is her own. Forget I said that. Ignore your mother, okay. She's just used to getting what she wants. *(Holding up his drink.)* Here's to USC.

MATT. What I wanted to say, the thing is, she doesn't really understand what's going on.

JERRY. You chose USC. She must be upset to say the least.

MATT. She doesn't know that.

JERRY. She doesn't know what?

MATT. That I decided on USC.

JERRY. You applied early decision.

MATT. She doesn't know.

JERRY. I'm not following this, Matt.

MATT. She thinks I applied to Stony Brook early decision.

JERRY. Why does she think that?

MATT. That's what I told her.

JERRY. I'm not following.

MATT. I told her I applied early decision to Stony Brook. I figured I would tell her the truth when I got in.

JERRY. When you got in?

MATT. Yeah. That way she won't be able to do anything. Once I get into USC, I'm legally bound to go, right? She'd be foiled.

JERRY. You're serious, aren't you?

MATT. Well, what did you want me to do? She would never have let me —

JERRY. What did I want you to do?! I wanted you to tell her the truth.

MATT. Why didn't you tell her? Why did I have to tell her?

JERRY. I can't tell her that. That's not my place. You have to tell her.

MATT. You don't understand. She doesn't want me to leave Long Island. Ever. She wants me to live in Sayville and watch the Smothers Brothers for the rest of my life.

JERRY. Matt, she's going to miss you. It's the empty nest syndrome. It's natural. But if you think your mother doesn't want you to go to the best college you can, you're crazy. Nothing means more to her than an education.

MATT. You don't understand. You're not there.

JERRY. When are you going to find out?

MATT. Any day now.

JERRY. Any day now? She could be opening the letter right now.

MATT. I check the mailbox, don't worry. She can't just wheel out and get the mail, Dad.

JERRY. What about the mail man? He could bring it inside for her.

MATT. I'm on top of it, Dad.

JERRY. Oh, Matt. Matt. This is not good.

MATT. Look, I'll talk to her tomorrow, okay. She'll want a whiskey sour 'cause it's Christmas eve. She's better when she's drunk.

JERRY. Well, get her good and goddamned soused then. And don't tell her this was my idea. I had *nothing* to do —

MATT. I know, I know. And you never saw the pen, either.

JERRY. Don't be smart like that. There are things going on that you don't understand. You know how to make a whiskey sour?

MATT. Yes.

JERRY. Good. Cause that's all she drinks. Whiskey sours. And don't let her eat anything first.

MATT. Okay.

JERRY. There used to be a bunch of those powder mixes in the kitchen drawer. I wish you had told me this before. There's a lot going on right now. This is the last thing we need. More bomb shells.

MATT. What's going on?

JERRY. Just a lot of things.

MATT. Like what?

JERRY. Look, I don't want to get into it now.

MATT. Why?

JERRY. Sally's being transferred, that's all.

MATT. She is? Where?

JERRY. Her whole company. They're moving everyone to Los Angeles.

MATT. What are you guys going to do?

JERRY. Well, it would be a pretty difficult thing to overcome, that kind of separation.

MATT. Are you going to break up?

JERRY. No. Of course not. We're ... we're finally getting married. *(Beat.)* I didn't want to get into this now.

MATT. I thought you were happy being a bachelor.

JERRY. Things change. She's a WASP. Her parents don't share my liberal view of things. They've been tough as hell on her. I have a lot of strikes against me with them. I'm older. I'm recently divorced. I'm a shrink. This is the least I can do — get married.

MATT. Where are you going to live?

JERRY. We'll talk about all this later.

MATT. Are you moving there, too?

JERRY. Matt —

MATT. You can't.

JERRY. I have to, Matt.

MATT. I'm the one going to California.

JERRY. I know. That's why I'm so excited.

MATT. I can't believe this.

JERRY. We'll be able to see each other.

MATT. I don't see you here. Why would I see you there?

JERRY. What are you saying? We see each other.

MATT. At funerals.

JERRY. We're having dinner.

MATT. Oh and now. Around Christmas. I forgot.

JERRY. Well, let's try to do better. We'll go watch the ball drop on New Year's Eve. You used to love to watch that on TV. Remember? We'd eat pizza and watch Guy Lombardo.

MATT. I can't believe you're doing this.

JERRY. You're overreacting.

MATT. Ouch.

JERRY. I thought you'd be happy.

MATT. Ouch.

JERRY. Are you alright?

MATT. It hurt when I swallowed.

JERRY. Are you getting sick or something?

MATT. No. The salad scratched my throat I think.

JERRY. Scratched your throat?

MATT. Yes.

JERRY. Why don't you drink some water. *(Matt does. He winces in pain.)* I don't think lettuce can do that, Matt.

MATT. It hurts. Okay. It hurts.

JERRY. Okay. Relax.

MATT. *(Sipping water.)* Ow. It's my esophagus.

JERRY. Your esophagus?

MATT. Yes. It's not my throat. It's lower down.

JERRY. You hurt your esophagus?

MATT. Yes.

JERRY. This is ridiculous. You can't damage your esophagus.

MATT. I just did.

JERRY. Wait a little while. Just breathe. I'm sure it will go away. Don't swallow for a moment.

MATT. *(Swallowing after a moment.)* Ouch.

JERRY. Just relax. I really don't think you can scratch your throat —

MATT. Esophagus.

JERRY. Your esophagus with a piece of lettuce.

MATT. Ouch.

JERRY. Look, clearly I've said something provocative. You're reacting to what I said.

MATT. No, I'm not.

JERRY. Yes, you are. You're having a hard time "swallowing what I'm saying." I'm a psychologist. I know these things. You internalize things. You get headaches when you're angry. What does Doctor Klein think about this?

MATT. He thinks you're scared of Mom.

JERRY. Oh. That's interesting. I don't see what it has to do with your problems, much less reality, but it's interesting.

MATT. You sent me to him. I'm just telling you what he said.

JERRY. You worry about your mother too much, Matt. I wish you'd just let her roll off your back.

MATT. You didn't. You just left her to me.

JERRY. I did not. I stayed. I stayed for years. I did that for you.

MATT. If you added it up, I've probably spent more time with her than you ever did.

JERRY. She's your mother and you're stuck with her. Okay. End of discussion. Do you see the waiter? I'd like another drink.

MATT. When were you going to tell her all this? Or do you want me to tell her that too?

JERRY. I'm going to talk to her. I wrote her a letter but you can only say so much in a letter. Did she get it yet?

MATT. Ouch.

JERRY. How could you have damaged your esophagus?

MATT. I don't know, but I did.

JERRY. You're too sensitive, Matt. You take too much on. Your mother's going to be fine. She can take care of herself, trust me. Do you know how much I've been sending her every month? A lot. Sometimes I worry, that you ... Look I'm not saying she created it, I'm just saying the mind and the body, they work as one. And, please, don't share this with your mother, but I think her attitude ... The way we look at the world, it affects our physical health. We have to be responsible for our bodies as well. The bottom line is, you're not your mother. You don't have what she has. You need to remind yourself of that. You don't have to hold yourself back on account of her. It's okay to move on. I want to give you permission to move on. You've got to have dreams, Matt. And you've got to believe they can come true. Let's go watch the ball drop next week. Your mother will find something to do, I promise. She's not as helpless as you think.

MATT. She's in a wheelchair.

JERRY. So was FDR. *(Beat.)*

MATT. *(Getting up.)* You know what? I'm not going to college.

JERRY. Matt.

MATT. *(Putting on his coat.)* I'm going to Vietnam to watch Bob Hope.

JERRY. Matt. I'm sorry, I … What are you doing?

MATT. You're right. I stole your Christmas present. *(Matt exits. Jerry sits alone. Fade to black.)*

Scene 3

Christmas Eve. The living room. Helen's in her wheelchair, a cocktail glass in hand. Matt stands nearby.

HELEN. I thought it was a Christmas card.

MATT. Ignore it.

HELEN. This is just great. You get a letter from your husband on Christmas eve, you just assume it's a Christmas card. It's not like it's a business size envelope. It's card size.

MATT. Throw it out.

HELEN. You get a car and I get a wedding announcement.

MATT. I'll return the car.

HELEN. A Volkswagon. It's like a swastika in my driveway.

MATT. How's that whiskey sour doing, mom?

HELEN. He can get married to this blond cocktail waitress shiksa if he wants. See if I care.

MATT. She's an executive secretary.

HELEN. Oh, please. What is that? If she's a secretary, she's a secretary. The fact that her boss is an executive, mazel tov to him. She's still a secretary.

MATT. How about another drink?

HELEN. When's dinner?

MATT. In a few minutes. Here, let me get you another. *(Matt takes her glass to the table where he has set up a little bar.)*

HELEN. Are you trying to get me drunk?

MATT. It's Christmas eve, come on.

HELEN. These pants are too tight. I look fat.

MATT. They look nice.

HELEN. They're too tight. I don't know why I even bother. How is anything supposed to fit if I can't try it on.

MATT. *(Returning with the drinks.)* You look great.

HELEN. I look awful.

MATT. *(Toasting.)* Merry Christmas.

HELEN. A Volkswagon.

MATT. I said I'll return it.

HELEN. Some things you don't forget. And it's not about being Jewish. We were never Jewish at this house. Do you remember when you were a child and the school nurse asked you what religion you were? What did you say?

MATT. Atheist.

HELEN. I told you to say agnostic, but atheist was fine. She called me, didn't she?

MATT. Well, she wanted to know my religion, not whether I believed in God.

HELEN. I went down there and took her head off. She regretted that call. When my father came to this country he wanted to be an American, not a Jew. He named my brother George Washington for Christ's sake. That's your uncle's name. George Washington Nevitz. That's what saves this country. The separation of church and state.

MATT. You should run for office.

HELEN. Me? I'm in a wheelchair.

MATT. So was FDR.

HELEN. They hid that. There was a time when you could hide things like that. Anyway, I'm not a candidate. If nominated I will not run, if elected I will not serve.

MATT. You can at least fantasize, can't you?

HELEN. Why bother?

MATT. Do you ever think about what you would do if you could walk?

HELEN. Walk? If I could walk I would … just … walk.

MATT. That would be nice.

HELEN. I used to take walks. For absolutely no reason.

MATT. You could go back to the Philharmonic. You could go even if there were no more aisle seats left.

HELEN. The Philharmonic? I would just be sitting down at the Philharmonic. I can do that just as well now.

29

MATT. So what would you do if you could walk? If you could do *anything* you want, what would you do?

HELEN. Well, I couldn't do *anything* I wanted, could I. I couldn't fly to the moon. Not that I ever would. It's a disgraceful waste of money.

MATT. Dad thinks we can find the answers to our problems in space.

HELEN. Send him then. That's a launch I'd be happy to pay for.

MATT. Why don't you get the Gardeners to take you to the Philharmonic?

HELEN. He's too fat!

MATT. Are you drunk yet?

HELEN. I'm tipsy.

MATT. Good.

HELEN. I would buy a pair of high-heeled shoes. Elegant shoes. When I was at school, I wore the most beautiful shoes in an absolutely fabulous production of *Uncle Tom's Cabin*.

MATT. You did?

HELEN. I was cast as Emily Shelby who is the plantation owner's wife and who, by the way, does not believe in slavery. She's one of the novel's many morally virtuous and insightful female characters, all of whom wear the most beautiful shoes. *(In a southern accent.)* "Uncle Tom, Harry, Eliza. It's Emily. Come with me right now. You are in mortal danger"

MATT. That's a good accent.

HELEN. Good Lord, now you've got me dreaming. Do you know what I'd really love to do? Take a bath. I haven't been completely submerged in water for ten years.

MATT. You could go to the beach and go swimming.

HELEN. No. I want bubbles. A bubble bath. I'd take a bubble bath in my high-heeled shoes. Oh, God. I would put a dress on. What a thought. I could wear dresses instead of pants with elastic waists for the rest of my life. My father used to love when I got dressed up. He would smile. And that man never smiled. Thank God he didn't live to see this.

MATT. See what?

HELEN. Me.

MATT. There's nothing wrong with you.

HELEN. I was someone once.

MATT. You still are.

HELEN. Barely. People stare at me now.

MATT. They stare at movie stars too.

HELEN. I'm an accident. They're rubberneckers craning to see the blood.

MATT. You're still someone. Stop it.

HELEN. Is that why you never invited Ian Chapman over here? Were you ashamed?

MATT. No.

HELEN. I wasn't always in this chair, you know. I used to have an office. Do you remember that? I had an office. With a nice view of Union Square. You don't remember.

MATT. It's not like you ever talk about it. *(Beat.)* I remember your office. I just don't remember you in it.

HELEN. Who do you think brought you there?

MATT. I can't remember you ever walking.

HELEN. Don't be ridiculous.

MATT. I can't.

HELEN. Have you told Doctor Klein this?

MATT. Dr. Klein told me to go up to the attic and look at the pictures. There's one of you and Dad on Martha's Vineyard holding a beach ball. Where did you guys meet?

HELEN. Some gin joint.

MATT. I'm serious.

HELEN. So am I. It was called The Blue Canary. Children. The things they don't know about their parents. I would go back there if it's still open. That's one of the first things I would do. We loved each other. We still do. I tell you something. If I hadn't gotten sick, he never would have left. But how would you know that? All you know is this. It's humiliating. Maybe I should have another drink. Clearly there's a stretch between tipsy and drunk I'm not enjoying.

MATT. Do you ever think the way we look at the world affects things? I mean, affects our physical health.

HELEN. No. Not at all.

MATT. Maybe if you had … some faith.

HELEN. Faith? Faith in what?

MATT. Not God. But something. Maybe things would get better. Maybe if you just had a better attitude.

HELEN. Have you lost your mind?

MATT. Alright, forget it. Just drop it. Let's eat.

HELEN. You haven't found one of those Eastern religions, have you? One of those Gurus?

MATT. I didn't find anything. Forget it. Let's open your presents.

HELEN. Yours hasn't gotten here yet.

MATT. That's okay.

HELEN. They promised delivery by today. *(Matt puts two gifts down next to her.)*

MATT. It's okay. I understand

HELEN. I ordered you a cardigan sweater and an earmuff from the L.L. Bean catalogue. They just didn't get here yet. *(Matt hands Helen a present.)*

MATT. Open this one first. *(She's unwrapped a book. Matt reenters with two plates, filled with food. He sets them on the table.)*

HELEN. What is this?

MATT. I read about it in Popular Science.

HELEN. *The Multiple Sclerosis Diet Book.*

MATT. There was a whole article about it. How promising it is. It's not a cure, but, there was this Norwegian study with a surprisingly large number of patients. It helped to stabilize things and in some cases even slow down the deterioration.

HELEN. I've already deteriorated, but thank you very much.

MATT. The recipes are pretty good. They have pot roast —

HELEN. I can only imagine.

MATT. I made one of them tonight. Ta da!

HELEN. What is it?

MATT. You have to admit it smells good.

HELEN. What is it?

MATT. Salisbury Steak with no added oil.

HELEN. This is your idea of a present? Dry Salisbury Steak?

MATT. And Pineapple Cottage Cheese Pie.

HELEN. And this is supposed to cure me?

MATT. Help you. I'm not making it up. It was in *Popular Science.*

HELEN. Science isn't popular. It's rigorous and difficult.

MATT. Then forget it. Eat what you want.

HELEN. It's not like I have a choice. That's what you made. *(Indicating the other present.)* What's this one?

MATT. Who cares?

HELEN. Oh, stop it. It's not your fault they publish these ridiculous books. *(Picking up the other present.)* What's in this one? *(Nothing from Matt.)* Don't get moody. It's not your fault. *(Helen is opening the other present.)*

MATT. You won't like it. *(Helen has it unwrapped. Beat.)* It's a camera. *(Helen puts it down.)* I thought we could take some pictures.

HELEN. You're right. I don't want it.

MATT. I saved up for it.

HELEN. It was too expensive, I'm sure.

MATT. *(Opening the box.)* Let me show you how it works.

HELEN. No.

MATT. Come on, it's simple. It has an automatic f-stop and everything.

HELEN. Put it back.

MATT. *(Pointing the camera at her.)* Look.

HELEN. *(Covering her face.)* No!

MATT. Okay. Okay.

HELEN. Put it back!

MATT. Okay! It's not a gun. *(Beat.)*

HELEN. I'm sorry. It's all these whiskey sours. I can't think straight. Take it to Stony Brook with you. Let's just eat. What did you make? It really does smell good. What is it?

MATT. Onion, garlic, oregano, black pepper, salt, burgundy wine and lean beef roast.

HELEN. Don't be mad. I'm sorry if I don't consider oregano to be the answer to all my problems.

MATT. You don't consider anything to be the answer to your problems. Except for me. I'm not going to be here forever, you know. Have you ever thought about this?

HELEN. You know what? I'm not hungry now.

MATT. What if Dad moved away? Have you ever considered any of this?

HELEN. As far as I can tell he already has.

MATT. Fine. Just pretend nothing's going to change. Just sit there and watch the news and do your crossword puzzles.

HELEN. I can't. I don't have my pen.

MATT. Forget about that stupid pen! You lost it! You lost it, you lost it, you lost it! People lose things.

HELEN. I don't. Where am I going to lose anything?

MATT. Maybe you left it at the beauty parlor.

HELEN. Why would I take a pen to the beauty parlor?

MATT. To do the crossword puzzle.

HELEN. Are you crazy? I have to concentrate. I have to watch him like a hawk, or I'll come back looking like Mamie Eisenhower.

MATT. Maybe Mrs. Green took your pen. Did you ask her?

HELEN. You sound like one of those horrible women who blames the poor maid every time they misplace a fork.

MATT. Sometimes maids do bad things. Maids aren't perfect just because they're maids.

HELEN. Believe me, I know. They can be all sorts of things. Mostly they're illiterate, which is not the same —

MATT. As stupid.

HELEN. That's right. But she didn't take my pen. She knows how much I need that pen.

MATT. Maybe she lost it. She's forgetful you said.

HELEN. I did not. I said she was distracted. She's lonely.

MATT. How do you know?

HELEN. Because they all are. Because they have to leave families in South Carolina and look for work.

MATT. She lives in the Bronx.

HELEN. At her sister's. You don't know. Her children are in South Carolina. She sends money to them every month.

MATT. I didn't know she had children.

HELEN. Well, now you know. Maybe you can treat her better.

MATT. I treat her fine. You're the one who bosses her around, who tells her exactly how to do everything.

HELEN. How's she supposed to know otherwise? She's illiterate.

MATT. I don't go around calling the maid illiterate.

HELEN. It's not her fault she's illiterate.

MATT. It's my fault, right. It's probably my fault.

HELEN. It's our fault.

MATT. Oh, my God. I WAS BEING SARCASTIC, OKAY? It's not my fault. In no way is it even part my fault. I'm a high school senior. I am not responsible for our maid's illiteracy.

HELEN. You have been taught in some of the finest classrooms —

MATT. Forgive me. Forgive me.

HELEN. We took you to concerts, theatre, the ballet. There are countless others who have had none of those advantages. In a larger sense, it is your fault. You took their place.

MATT. There's not one place. I'm not stopping anyone.

HELEN. *(Staring at the coffee table.)* I'm missing a refill. One of my refills is gone.

MATT. What?

HELEN. You heard me.

MATT. What do you mean, one of your refills is gone?

HELEN. That's what I'm asking you. The refills are only good for one pen.

MATT. How do you know one's missing? There are a ton of them there.

HELEN. There are eleven. There should be twelve. I know that because I can't get them anymore. The company's out of business. I told you. I bought as many refills as they had left. I tried to prepare. I had twelve refills left. I use a refill a year, approximately. That would have given me twelve years. Approximately. I had twelve years left. That's how I know. Because it matters. Do you think Mrs. Green stole it? Is that what you think? Do you think she took the pen back to her sister's one room apartment and wrote all night about what it's like to not know how to read? Do you think she had so much to write she ran out of ink, drove down here and stole one of my refills, all the while not realizing she doesn't have a neuromuscular disease and doesn't need this one particular pen to write lying down with? She could have saved herself all the trouble and walked down to her local five and dime and bought any old pen for about twenty-five cents.

MATT. I don't know what you want me to say.

HELEN. How long have you had my pen?

MATT. I don't have it.

HELEN. It's one thing to steal. That's bad enough. But to implicate a maid. How low can you get?

MATT. You don't care about the fucking maid. You just want me to feel guilty.

HELEN. Of course I care.

MATT. Fuck you.

HELEN. Language doesn't shock me, sorry.

MATT. Fuck you. You make me feel just to *want* something is wrong.

HELEN. You can swear all night.

MATT. Nigger!

HELEN. How dare you talk like that.

MATT. Nigger!

HELEN. Oh, my God.

MATT. Nigger! Nigger! Nigger!

HELEN. Stop it! You're scaring me now.

MATT. You don't care about black people. You don't care about anyone but yourself. You know what? I've changed my mind. Dad was right. You're not worth worrying about. I'm going to college! In California! I've applied. Early decision. And not to Stony Brook. I wrote the whole application with your pen. There, are you happy now?! And I used up every drop of ink to do it. And then I typed it on Dad's typewriter. I don't need any more refills. It's over. I hope

I never see you again for the rest of my life. *(Beat.)* Say something!

HELEN. You did this on your father's typewriter?

MATT. And he's moving to California with me! He's getting re-married and moving to California where we're all going to live.

HELEN. You don't think you're actually going to get in, do you?

MATT. Yes, I do.

HELEN. You have a police record.

MATT. They're never going to find that out.

HELEN. You lied on your application?

MATT. I didn't lie. Dad said —

HELEN. Your father's a fool. Of course they'll find out.

MATT. How?

HELEN. Because I'm going to tell them. *(She wheels over to the phone.)* You two may feel comfortable lying on a —

MATT. They didn't ask about that.

HELEN. Of course they asked. They all ask. Somewhere between your name and your birthplace.

MATT. They asked about felonies.

HELEN. They ask if you were arrested, not for what. *(Helen picks up the phone.)*

MATT. Who are you calling?

HELEN. Information. I'm going to get the phone number for the admissions office.

MATT. I'm not staying here!

HELEN. This is why I talked to them at Stony Brook. I paved the way for you. *(Into the phone.)* Yes, I'd like the number for —

MATT. NO! *(Matt grabs the phone from her.)*

HELEN. Give me that phone! I am not going to be privy to a lie!

MATT. You don't want me to leave!

HELEN. This is for your own good.

MATT. No, it's for yours. Everything's for yours. You sit there in the middle of the house! You never leave! I can hear you clear your throat from my bedroom!

HELEN. I can hear you, too, and you're not clearing your throat!

MATT. Oh, my God!

HELEN. Give me the phone.

MATT. Here! Take it! *(Matt throws the phone at her. It crashes to the floor and breaks.)* This must be what Andy Lyons felt.

HELEN. Don't say that.

MATT. I give up. Here, take your pen. I give up. Take it. *(Matt takes out the pen and puts it down on the coffee table in front of her.*

Matt sits down on the floor.) Take my legs. Please. Walk! Go on, walk!

HELEN.   How dare you mock me. Get up.

MATT.   No.

HELEN.   You're being a fool. Get up. I mean it. Get up.

MATT.   No. WALK! *(Silence. Helen ever so slowly stands up. She lets out a small gasp. Matt stands up. They face each other for a few seconds before Matt falls to the ground. Fade to black.)*

End of Act One

ACT TWO

Scene 1

December 30. Evening. An old New York City bar. Darkly lit. Jerry sits at a small table nursing a drink. After a while he takes his martini and leaves. Helen comes in. She wears a blond wig, large sunglasses, and high-heeled shoes. She carries a bunch of shopping bags. She looks around. She takes her overcoat off, draping it over a chair, revealing a lovely dress. She removes her sunglasses. She walks up to a mirror and looks at herself. She eventually sits down at the same table Jerry was at. She takes in the room. She removes a compact from her purse and powders herself. She takes lipstick out. Jerry comes back.

JERRY. Excuse me. I think I was sitting there. *(Helen looks up. She quickly shoves the lip stick back in her purse.)* I was just using the pay-phone. *(Helen talks very softly, holding her hand up to her face.)*
HELEN. Sorry. *(Helen grabs her jacket off the chair, keeping her head down.)*
JERRY. It's okay. Stay. I took my glass with me. Simple misunderstanding. I didn't want the barkeep to grab it. *(Helen has managed to gather everything up and starts for the door.)* Excuse me. You forgot your sunglasses.
HELEN. Thanks. *(Helen, her head still lowered, walks back and takes them from Jerry. She immediately puts them back on and heads for the door.)*
JERRY. You're not a movie star are you?
HELEN. *(Very softly.)* No.
JERRY. Pardon me? *(Helen shakes her head.)* I'm kidding. You seem like you don't want to be recognized. *(Helen shrugs.)* You can join me if you want. I didn't mean to —
HELEN. It's late.
JERRY. I'm sorry? *(Helen touches her watch.)* I see. Well. *(Jerry sits down at the table. Helen finds herself still standing there.)* You live

around here? *(Helen nods her head no.)* I'm way down in the Village. You sure you won't join me? One drink? *(Helen doesn't respond but she doesn't leave either. Off her high-heeled shoes:)* Nice shoes. Christmas present?

HELEN. Mm, mm.

JERRY. I did pretty well this year. Although my son bought me ... well, he stole me a Lester Young album which I already had. I can't very well return it though, can I? You have any children? *(Helen shakes her head.)* Married?

HELEN. Not anymore.

JERRY. Sorry. *(Coyly.)* Although, maybe I shouldn't be. Where you from?

HELEN. *(In a southern accent.)* South Carolina.

JERRY. Excuse me.

HELEN. South Carolina.

JERRY. Did you go to the university there?

HELEN. No.

JERRY. The Gamecocks. They're not Pac-10 but they're good. Can I buy you a drink?

HELEN. I don't think so.

JERRY. Come on, take a load off. Relax. I'm just settling in myself.

HELEN. Um ... Well ... Alright. One. I'll have a whiskey sour.

JERRY. I'll be right back. *(Jerry leaves for the bar. Helen looks at herself in the mirror. She adjusts her wig.)*

HELEN. *(Practicing her accent.)* "Uncle Tom, Harry, Eliza. Come with me right now. You are in mortal danger." *(Jerry returns with the drinks.)*

JERRY. One whiskey sour coming right up. Women love that drink, huh?

HELEN. Well, some do, some don't.

JERRY. My ex-wife, that's all she drinks. That and blood. Just kidding. *(Sitting back down.)* Are you ever going to sit down?

HELEN. Maybe. *(Helen lays her coat on the back of a chair. She sits at the table next to Jerry's.)*

JERRY. Okay, if that's the way you want it.

HELEN. I do.

JERRY. Jerry.

HELEN. Emily. Emily Shelby.

JERRY. So, is it true blonds have more fun?

HELEN. Excuse me? *(Remembering her wig.)* Oh.

JERRY. I always liked that ad. I like commercials. So? Do they have more fun?

HELEN. I'll let you know. How about that?

JERRY. "I'll let you know." Very funny. I'm going to tell you straight up. I like women like you. Feisty.

HELEN. Thanks. I guess.

JERRY. So, Emily, what are you doing tomorrow. You have plans for New Year's Eve?

HELEN. Not really. And you?

JERRY. I'm not sure. My ... well, she's my fiancée — I have to get used to that — She's in Los Angeles. So, I thought I'd take my thieving son to see the ball drop in Times Square.

HELEN. I see.

JERRY. I haven't confirmed it yet. I keep calling.

HELEN. Where does he live?

JERRY. With his mother.

HELEN. What about her reminds you of a blood sucker?

JERRY. Oh, nothing. Just kidding. Just kidding.

HELEN. I thought there was a little truth to every joke.

JERRY. Helen is a powerhouse, that's all. Helen. It's such a straightforward name, isn't it? So direct. I kept trying to give her a nickname, you know, soften it up. All I came up with was Hell.

HELEN. I see. What's your fiancée like?

JERRY. Oh, the best. She's the best.

HELEN. The best. Wow. Why?

JERRY. Gosh, she's special. I don't know.

HELEN. What's special about her?

JERRY. You sound like my high school girlfriend. She kept wanting to know, "But why do you like me? Why?" Okay, you know why she's so special? She loves me.

HELEN. Is that so special of her? You don't seem all that unlovable.

JERRY. You don't know. *(Beat.)* You look familiar.

HELEN. I sincerely doubt that.

JERRY. I see a lot of people in my job, so you never know. I'm a psychologist. Actually, I have a book coming out. It's a self help book.

HELEN. Self help?

JERRY. I know. Publishers are using the term. It's about believing we can all be whatever we want to be if we can just believe it.

HELEN. We could all use a little help doing that.

JERRY. Oh, you have no idea. People sabotage themselves constantly. I could tell you stories. The thing you learn in my line of work is, nothing is what it seems. Like you're wearing sunglasses in

40

a dimly lit bar. At night. I'm not even going to ask why.

HELEN. They're prescription. I left my clear ones at home.

JERRY. I'm not buying it. But that's my job description. I've got to dig deeper. For instance, why do you think I asked an attractive woman to have a drink with me?

HELEN. I don't know.

JERRY. Neither do I. Exactly. But at least I'm not trying to kid myself. I know there's something going on here.

HELEN. Sabotage?

JERRY. Feisty. *(Off his drink.)* To tell you the truth, I think I'm just drunk. This is my third. I can barely see straight.

HELEN. Lucky me.

JERRY. My wife, my ex-wife, we wrote a poem together once. It was about her being always late. Do you want to hear it?

HELEN. Yes.

JERRY. We wrote it sort of in the style of Dorothy Parker. Know her?

HELEN. Sure.

JERRY. It's about me always waiting for her at a bar and you know, drinking. *(Like Dorothy Parker.)* I don't know why she's always late, that's just the way it is. I've sort of come to count on it, much like my sloe gin fizz. I don't know what I'd ever do if this should ever change. But there's lots of liquor at the bar and nuts to rearrange.

HELEN. That's very clever.

JERRY. She's the one who mostly wrote it.

HELEN. That's big of you to admit.

JERRY. Oh, yeah. Well, she was the clever one. Clever like a fox.

HELEN. Foxes and blood suckers. You're very anthropomorphic when it comes to your ex-wife.

JERRY. Anthropomorphic. You're a crack up. I do a pretty good Dorothy Parker, though, don't I?

HELEN. Yes, you do.

JERRY. Ah, well. *(Silence.)*

HELEN. I haven't been here in such a long time.

JERRY. You've been to this gin joint.

HELEN. What? No, no. I meant the city. I haven't been to the city in a very long time.

JERRY. I grew up here. I came back after the war.

HELEN. Is this where you met Sally? New York City?

JERRY. Yeah. The Philharmonic.

HELEN. You still go to the Philharmonic?

JERRY. Old fashioned of me, isn't it?

HELEN. Sounds lovely.

JERRY. Yeah. *(Beat.)* Did I mention Sally?

HELEN. Your fiancée.

JERRY. I know. I wasn't sure I said her name.

HELEN. Oh. You did. When are you getting married.

JERRY. Next month. California. Ever been?

HELEN. No.

JERRY. I went to college there. USC.

HELEN. Oh.

JERRY. The problem is I have to get there.

HELEN. To the altar?

JERRY. No. To California. I hate to fly. But fly I will. Our relationship's been extremely awkward for her. The first few years we were sneaking around. Nobody even knew.

HELEN. You mean your wife.

JERRY. Right. Anyway, now we're living together. And she comes from a very, very conservative family. All this out of wedlock stuff is killing them. They've been as cold as ice to her. These are diehard Republicans. I mean, they voted for Goldwater.

HELEN. Oh, no, Jerry.

JERRY. She thought a wedding might thaw them out a little.

HELEN. Your fiancée voted for Goldwater?

JERRY. No. Her parents did.

HELEN. These things trickle down.

JERRY. *(Laughing.)* You sound like my first wife.

HELEN. I'm sorry. I wouldn't want to do that.

JERRY. I keep calling Long Island. Nobody picks up. Which is very odd. I'm starting to think it's a ploy to get me over there.

HELEN. You're the psychologist.

JERRY. Well, I got to go anyway. I'm just generating the courage. Maybe that's what I'm doing here. Generating courage. I haven't been back since I left. I sent her a letter explaining, you know, that we were getting married.

HELEN. How thoughtful of you.

JERRY. I was trying to break the ice a little. But the timing turns out to be … My son — it seems he applied to USC without telling his mother. I'm not going to bore you with the details. I bought the kid a Karmen Gia too, which really pissed her off.

HELEN. Why?

JERRY. Apparently Hitler designed the damn thing. Who knew. She did. She can be very intimidating sometimes. It's probably why

I married her. She's very impressive.

HELEN. That's a good thing, isn't it?

JERRY. Yes and no. There are so many things about her that … God, this is like the proverbial stranger in a bar scene. My wife … my ex-wife. She has MS.

HELEN. I'm sorry.

JERRY. Thanks. It's been very hard on me. *(Beat.)* That's not something I say to many people. They would laugh at you. I can say it to you. You're a stranger. We went camping ten years ago on Martha's Vineyard. That's when it started. When I really started to notice it. I was walking around tonight — Sally's in Los Angles — I was going to go to this jazz club downtown, but I ended up here. This is where we met. By the jukebox. My ex-wife. "Of all the gin joints in all the towns in all the world … "

JERRY and HELEN. " … she walks into mine." *(Beat.)*

HELEN. Want another?

JERRY. If you have one. *(Helen leaves for the bar. Jerry goes over to the mirror. He takes out a comb and combs his hair. He sits back down. Helen comes back with two drinks.)*

HELEN. Another Whiskey Sour. And one martini. Extra dry.

JERRY. How did you know?

HELEN. The bartender told me.

JERRY. Pete. Makes a great martini.

HELEN. Cheers.

JERRY. Cheers. *(They drink.)* Oh, God. What am I doing here? I'm about to get married.

HELEN. I don't know. Maybe you still have feelings for her. Your first wife.

JERRY. Yeah. My son's angry at me, you know. I think all this shoplifting … He was arrested for shoplifting. He thinks I deserted his mother. And deserted him, too. When I went to pick Matt up at the police station … That's my son, Matt. They told me he had shoved a shirt down his pants. That's all it was. A shirt. They showed it to me. I noticed it was a woman's shirt. The buttons were on the wrong side. He doesn't have a girlfriend. I think it was for his mom. He tells me she's so upset she never gets to go shopping anymore. I think the shirt was for her. I know it was. It's funny, I think about the house a lot. Why do we care so much about the houses we lived in? I suppose they symbolize a lot of hope. Families. People living together. Sally, she's such a WASP. She's not the best talker, but she listens. Or maybe it just appears that way. Maybe she's really thinking about her tennis game with Buffy, I don't know. With Helen and me ... we both talk a lot. We're Jews. Actually, I'm only half Jewish. My father's a Jew, my mother's a WASP: I feel nothing, but I feel guilty about it. Sorry, just a shrink joke. Helen's father, when he found out I had Episcopalian blood, he loved that. Her father was a ... Well, he was an anti-Semite. Can we just admit it? A Jewish anti-Semite. I think Helen's father hated himself in general. He was a hard man to please. The whole family's hard to please. She would have killed for your hair. We'd come in here a lot. She'd have, you know, a whiskey sour and I'd do martinis. I don't know what happened. We ended up on Long Island at Phil and Bebe Krugman's Sukkoth party. You probably don't even know what Sukkoth is?

HELEN. Vaguely.

JERRY. It's just a lot of Brussel sprouts and cauliflower. It's so suburban. I felt so trapped.

HELEN. Maybe if you had told your wife. Maybe she felt trapped too.

JERRY. It wouldn't have made a difference.

HELEN. You never know. *(Beat.)* Would you have left her, if...? If she...?

JERRY. If she hadn't gotten sick? What difference does it make? People believe what they want.

HELEN. I wouldn't question you.

JERRY. It wouldn't be easy to admit you left someone because they ended up in a wheelchair. It's like leaving a wounded animal.

HELEN. Is that what you did?

JERRY. I don't know.

HELEN. It might be easier for her if that was the case.

JERRY. Why?

HELEN. It's something that happened. It's not her fault then. There's hope.

JERRY. Christ, what am I doing here? *(Helen gets up and goes to the jukebox. She takes a quarter out and drops it in. She chooses a song. An old standard. She moves to the center of the room. Jerry gets up and goes over to her. They start to dance. It's beautiful to watch. The music begins to slow down. Something's wrong with the machine. Finally, the music stops altogether.)* It's an old machine.

HELEN. I should go.

JERRY. Why?

HELEN. Thanks for the dance.

JERRY. You're very good.

44

HELEN. Hardly.

JERRY. You are.

HELEN. It's been a long time.

JERRY. That's a shame. You're so good.

HELEN. You don't know. *(They're standing very close.)*

JERRY. You smell very ...

HELEN. What?

JERRY. Nothing. You want to get out of here? We'll grab a nightcap somewhere else.

HELEN. That's quite an invitation.

JERRY. I hope you don't think I —

HELEN. No. Of course not.

JERRY. You asked me to dance, right.

HELEN. If you don't mind me saying so, maybe you shouldn't do it.

JERRY. Just a nightcap. Scouts honor.

HELEN. I mean get married.

JERRY. Yeah. Right. Of course.

HELEN. I should go home.

JERRY. Right. Of course. No, you're right. *(Helen goes back to the table and gathers her things.)* Thank God for women and their second thoughts. Men don't have second thoughts. We just have the first one over and over again. I should write a book about that. I should write a book about a lot of things.

HELEN. Good night, Jerry.

JERRY. What about you?

HELEN. Excuse me?

JERRY. Why don't we skip the dark glasses at night bit and you just tell me why you left your husband.

HELEN. I didn't. He left me.

JERRY. Why would anyone do that?

HELEN. I don't know. Have any ideas? *(Helen starts to leave and then turns around.)* Maybe you're right. Maybe Helen isn't answering the phone for a reason. Maybe it's a ploy. You should go over there anyway. I'm sure your son would love to see you. *(Helen leaves. Jerry sits alone. The jukebox suddenly starts working again. Fade to black.)*

Scene 2

Later that night. Matt, in pajamas, has a glass of milk wedged between his legs. He slowly wheels himself across the room, careful not to spill it. He gets to the coffee table and puts the glass of milk within reaching distance of the sofa. He wheels closer to the sofa and locks the brakes to the wheelchair. Using his arms, he gets himself up on his legs. He puts one hand on the side of the couch, pivots and falls back on the couch. He reaches to get the remote control, but knocks it on the floor instead. It is out of reach of where he's sitting. Matt reaches for the wheelchair. He unlocks the brakes so he can position it correctly. He puts one hand on the arm of the couch and one on the arm of the wheelchair, rocks, and gets back into the wheelchair. He rolls over and retrieves the remote control from the floor, stuffing it down his pants. He wheels back over to the couch. He locks the brakes and attempts the same thing he did before to get back on the couch. But this time, as he pivots, he doesn't get far enough around, and lands on the coffee table.

MATT. Damn. *(He inadvertently knocks the glass of milk over with his hand. From the coffee table he attempts to get back into the chair, putting his hands on both arms of it, but he can't pivot enough and falls to the ground. Helen comes in. She doesn't see him on the floor. She's still in her wig and has shopping bags.)* Where have you been?
HELEN. Matt. What happened?
MATT. What do you think happened?
HELEN. Hold on. *(Helen puts her bags down. She goes over to help him up.)* What am I stepping in?
MATT. Milk.
HELEN. Oh, Matt. *(Helen goes to pick him up.)*
MATT. *(Pushing her away.)* Don't touch me. I don't need your help.
HELEN. Fine. I'll get some paper towels. *(She goes into the kitchen. Meanwhile, Matt tries to get off the floor and back into the chair. Helen returns with the paper towels.)*
MATT. Where were you?
HELEN. I was out.

MATT. It's one o'clock in the morning.

HELEN. I'm sorry. I missed the earlier train. I don't know what you were trying to do in here.

MATT. I was trying to drink some milk. Do you mind? *(Helen bends down to mop up the spilt milk.)*

HELEN. What happened? You should be able to manage a glass of milk.

MATT. What happened when you were on the bathroom floor with your pants down to your ankles?

HELEN. I had a fever of a hundred and two.

MATT. Well, who do you think pulled your pants up and lifted you back up?

HELEN. Alright, that's enough. *(Gathers up the groceries.)* Did you have dinner?

MATT. No, I didn't have dinner.

HELEN. Are you hungry?

MATT. No. I'm still picturing you on the bathroom floor.

HELEN. Oh, get off your high horse. I changed your diapers.

MATT. Oh, my God! There's no comparison.

HELEN. Can I please help you up?

MATT. Leave me alone. Go! I mean it.

HELEN. Fine. Just lie there. *(Helen goes into the kitchen with the wet paper towels. Matt gives up trying to get back into the chair. He reaches and retrieves the remote control. He aims it and clicks. The TV comes on. A commercial selling Jello. Reentering:)* Please turn that thing off. *(Matt turns it up instead.)* You know what? I can just leave the room. *(Helen goes back into the kitchen. The Jello commercial ends. Next is one for Salem cigarettes. Matt turns it up even louder. Helen comes back from the kitchen.)* Okay, I'm not going to listen to a cigarette commercial. I mean it. Turn it off.

MATT. *(Singing along.)* "You can take Salem out of the country, but … You can't take the country out of Salem."

HELEN. Give me the remote control.

MATT. No.

HELEN. Give it to me.

MATT. *(Continues singing along.)* "You can take Salem out of the country, but … You can't take the country out of Salem." *(Helen walks over and unplugs the TV.)* I would never have done that to you.

HELEN. It's not the same. I have to teach you values. That's what mothers do.

MATT. You couldn't be a mother if you tried.

HELEN. I think you have a completely unrealistic view of mother-hood.

MATT. How's my car drive?

HELEN. Fine.

MATT. It must not have a lot of pickup with the weight of six million dead Jews on board.

HELEN. Mine was low on gas. I had to get to the train station.

MATT. Hypocrite.

HELEN. You're just being spiteful now. *(Matt tries to get back into the chair again. He struggles valiantly.)* Let me help you.

MATT. No! *(Matt continues to struggle.)*

HELEN. Matt.

MATT. I can do it myself.

HELEN. No, you can't. I can't watch this. *(Watching him.)* For God's sake. Sit up.

MATT. Alright, alright.

HELEN. I'm just putting my hands under your armpits, and lifting a little, alright?

MATT. Fine.

HELEN. There. Okay? Are you ready? One, two —

MATT. Don't rush me.

HELEN. I'm not rushing you.

MATT. Move closer.

HELEN. I am closer. Are you ready? One, two —

MATT. You're pinching my skin.

HELEN. Come on. One, two, three. *(Struggling to lift him.)* How much do you weigh?

MATT. No! I want to be in the wheelchair!

HELEN. You're just going to plug the TV back in and watch commercials. *(She succeeds in getting him onto the sofa and then sits in the wheelchair, resting.)* I heard of a woman — I'm sure this is apocryphal — a woman who discovered her child trapped under a car and somehow mustered the strength to lift the car with nothing but her bare hands. She rescued him. Do you think that's possible?

MATT. I hope you're not comparing yourself to her.

HELEN. You don't weigh as much as a car, but —

MATT. She saved him. The point of that story is she saved him. *(Beat.)*

HELEN. I bought some more Oreos. *(Helen takes a bag of Oreos from one of the shopping bags.)*

MATT. When are you going to fix the phone?

HELEN. You're the one who broke it.

MATT. I'm supposed to go to Doctor Klein tomorrow.

HELEN. On New Year's Eve? Nonsense. Can we just enjoy the holidays, please. You want an Oreo?

MATT. No.

HELEN. Oh, for Christ's sake, have an Oreo. *(She tosses him an Oreo. She takes one too. They both eat.)* I bought some frozen pizza too. I know you and your father love pizza on New Year's eve.

MATT. We like real pizza. From the pizzeria.

HELEN. Well, have what you want, then. *(Off the Oreo.)* I can't believe you don't like them when they get stale. They taste like brownies when they're stale.

MATT. Are you ever going to take that wig off? It looks ridiculous.

HELEN. I happen to like it. *(She tosses him another Oreo. They eat.)*

MATT. Where were you?

HELEN. I had a drink in the city.

MATT. Did you go to The Blue Canary.

HELEN. Yes.

MATT. By yourself?

HELEN. Women can go to bars alone now. Times have changed.

MATT. They probably thought you were a prostitute.

HELEN. That's a charming thing to say to your mother.

MATT. Have you taken a bath?

HELEN. Not yet. I bought some Calgon though. *(Beat.)*

MATT. This can't go on forever, you know. *(Beat.)* Just tell me how much more time you want?

HELEN. I read a book once. *Black Like Me.* You had to read that in English class, remember? He took this medication and exposed his entire body to ultraviolet rays to change his skin color, and then, looking as black as the night, he went into the world to learn what it was like to be reviled. Do you remember this story? It's like that for me. Only the inverse. I knew what that was like. But then, I put this wig on and stood in front of the mirror. I saw the face and body of a beautiful stranger. My legs were shapely. Even after years of atrophy, they were … lovely. Long and … pretty. Do you know what I did today? I walked. That's all. I just walked. And people smiled. No one smiled before, they just stared. You won't believe what happened at The Blue Canary.

MATT. What?

HELEN. A man looked at me in that way. I never thought a man would do that again.

MATT. Did you talk?

HELEN. Yes. It was lovely. I didn't remind him of all the bad things that can happen in life. We danced. Oh, boy.

MATT. Are you crying?

HELEN. If I had had more time, Matt, I swear … Oh, well. My taxi cab was going to turn into a pumpkin, wasn't it? *(She takes off her high-heeled shoes. Holding one up:)* Maybe I should have left one of these behind? *(She tosses the shoe away.)*

MATT. It's okay if you want to go out. Just let me know so I don't worry.

HELEN. You know what I would like to do? I'd like to go in and see Carson tape his show.

MATT. That would be fun.

HELEN. I'd have to see who he was going to have on first, but you're right, it could be fun.

MATT. Paula Prentiss was on tonight.

HELEN. Really. I always thought she was a he.

MATT. Why?

HELEN. She's been on before, you know. I was so shocked when Johnny brought her in. I thought it was Paul Aprentiss. *(They laugh.)*

MATT. She was talking about *Catch-22*. She's in it.

HELEN. You read that book, too.

MATT. We're supposed to read *A Separate Peace* next semester.

HELEN. There's homosexual undertones in that, you know.

MATT. I didn't.

HELEN. You'll see. And make sure that teacher of yours points that out to the class.

MATT. How am I going to go back to school? *(Beat.)* I'm not saying it has to be next week.

HELEN. Can I just enjoy this night? What's left of it. *(Beat.)*

MATT. Do you ever think we're the same person?

HELEN. We were once. You were a beautiful baby. You cried a lot, but that's what babies do. I liked you better when you were a little older. When we could have conversations. You and I could talk a blue streak.

MATT. I don't remember.

HELEN. You don't remember? We talked about everything. Colors, cows. I tucked you in at night. I read to you.

MATT. I remember *Charlotte's Web*.

HELEN. You cried like a baby. What did she write with her web over the pen? Do you remember that?

MATT. Some pig.

HELEN. You cried when she did that.

MATT. I cried because I asked you if Charlotte was going to heaven and you said, "Don't make me laugh."

HELEN. I'm sure I didn't say "don't make me laugh."

MATT. You told me there was no such thing as heaven.

HELEN. I might have said that.

MATT. You left me all alone in the universe with a dead spider.

HELEN. Is that all you remember? Sad things? It's not nice that you don't remember me when ... It's mean.

MATT. I don't do it on purpose.

HELEN. It's alright. I'm going to bring down the pictures from the attic, how about that? *(Beat.)* Hey, let's get you another glass of milk. We can dunk the Oreos. These are too fresh. How are you feeling? You didn't hurt yourself, did you?

MATT. No. My legs are twitching.

HELEN. I'm sorry. There's nothing you can do about that.

MATT. Can you stretch them?

HELEN. Of course. *(Helen goes over and rubs his feet.)*

MATT. I remember we were waiting for Dad to get the car. We were on the beach and it was taking so long so we started walking. And when we got off the sand, the path got a little rocky. There were pebbles, and when we stepped on them, they dug in. But it didn't really hurt, you said. You said it felt like small electrical shocks were running up your body. And when we got off the path the parking lot was hot. But you didn't want to put your flip-flops on. You said you liked the way the hot tar felt on your soles. It might be the last time. But then it got even too hot for you and you said, screw this. You ran all the way back to your car in your flip-flops. I chased you. We were laughing really hard. Dad wanted to know what was so funny.

HELEN. I remember that, too. *(Beat.)* See, that wasn't so hard. *(Fade to black.)*

Scene 3

The next evening. New Year's Eve. Matt, still in pajamas, sits in the wheelchair looking out the window.

HELEN. *(Offstage.)* What's going on?

MATT. He's just sitting there.

HELEN. *(Offstage.)* Is the engine still running?

MATT. Yes.

HELEN. *(Offstage.)* Well, he didn't come all the way out here just to turn around and go home.

MATT. How do you know?

HELEN. *(Offstage.)* I just do. *(Helen comes in with an ice bucket. A bottle of champagne is in it. She is dressed up but not wearing her wig.)* Don't stare like that. A watched pot never boils

MATT. Yes, it does. I've tried it. I put a pot of water on the stove and —

HELEN. It's just an expression.

MATT. It boiled.

HELEN. *(Getting a sweater.)* Here, your cardigan sweater from L.L. Bean finally came. I took all the tags off. Would you at least put this on please. *(Helen adjusts the bottle of champagne in the bucket.)* I put the pizza in. And we have some good French champagne.

MATT. Why are you trying to impress him?

HELEN. I'm not.

MATT. He's not staying. He just wants to take me to see the ball drop.

HELEN. What's he doing?

MATT. Nothing. He's just sitting there.

HELEN. He's generating courage.

MATT. He's getting out of the car.

HELEN. He is?

MATT. He's coming in. *(Helen straightens up the room.)*

HELEN. Matt, I want you to let me do all the talking. Do you understand?

MATT. Don't worry. You think I want to explain this? *(The doorbell rings.)*

HELEN. Come in.

MATT. Mom! *(Jerry comes in. He's carrying a bottle of champagne.)*

JERRY. Hey.

HELEN. Jerry. We saw your car.

JERRY. How are you?

HELEN. I'm fine.

JERRY. *(To Matt.)* Hi. *(Nothing from Matt.)* I didn't mean to just pop in like this.

HELEN. It certainly is a surprise.

JERRY. I've been calling. Are you guys alright?

HELEN. Yeah.

JERRY. Nobody picks up.

HELEN. There's something wrong with the phone.

JERRY. Is it fixed?

HELEN. We're trying.

JERRY. You have to get it fixed. It's dangerous to —

HELEN. It's the holidays. They're coming Friday.

MATT. Why weren't you worried if nobody picked up?

JERRY. I was.

MATT. Then why didn't you come over?

JERRY. I did. I'm here, aren't I?

MATT. Finally.

HELEN. Matt.

JERRY. It's alright. He's mad. He can be mad. It's okay. Let him be mad. I brought you guys some champagne. It's chilled.

HELEN. Thank you. Happy New Year.

JERRY. Happy New Year. *(Beat.)* Gosh. It looks exactly the same in here. Nothing's changed.

MATT. Not that you can see.

HELEN. Matt.

JERRY. Are you feeling okay? *(Matt doesn't answer.)* You had a pretty bad sore throat before Christmas.

MATT. Esophagus.

HELEN. He's been a little under the weather.

MATT. That's putting it mildly.

JERRY. *(Notices the ice bucket.)* I guess you guys are all set.

HELEN. It's French.

JERRY. I can see that. *(Off his bottle.)* I'll just put this crap in the icebox then.

HELEN. Why don't you open it?

JERRY. No, it's lousy. Save it for a rainy day.

HELEN. Then let's open ours.

JERRY. I don't have time to —

HELEN. Just one glass.

JERRY. It's too good to open now.

HELEN. That's what it's there for.

JERRY. Alright, fine. One glass. *(Jerry gets the French champagne and begins to uncork it.)* I assume he finally talked to you, right?

MATT. I gave her whiskey sours, just like you said.

JERRY. I had no idea he didn't tell you. If I had known —

HELEN. It's not your fault.

JERRY. If I had known ... Excuse me?

HELEN. It's not your fault. He's a child. He doesn't always think.

JERRY. Well, anyway. I'm sorry it happened like this. I'm glad you're being so understanding. Has he heard anything yet? Have you heard anything?

MATT. I don't know. Have I?

HELEN. No, he hasn't. Not yet.

JERRY. I'm sure it's going to be any day now. *(Jerry pops the cork. He fills the champagne flutes. He hands Helen and Matt their flutes.)*

HELEN. *(Toasting.)* Cheers.

JERRY. Cheers. *(They all drink.)*

HELEN. So, how are you?

JERRY. Me? Good. Good.

HELEN. You look good.

JERRY. Thank you. You too.

HELEN. Thanks. You must be looking forward to the Rose Bowl.

JERRY. I am, yes. Thank you. The Wolverines coach just had a heart attack this morning.

HELEN. Goodness.

JERRY. Should be an interesting game. *(They drink.)* So. Matty and I talked about maybe going to see the ball drop.

MATT. I told you.

JERRY. You want to go?

HELEN. I think it's a little too much for him right now. He's really not feeling —

JERRY. Oh, come on. It's the end of a decade.

HELEN. Why don't we just watch the ball on TV? It'll be like old times.

JERRY. It's not the same on TV. *(To Matt.)* Come on. Let's go. It's an incredible spectacle.

HELEN. I put a pizza in the oven.

JERRY. Pizza.

MATT. It's Chef Boy-R-Dee.

JERRY. What's the matter with Mario's?

MATT. The phone's not working.

JERRY. That's dangerous.

MATT. Then fix it, if it's so dangerous.

JERRY. I'm not a telephone repair man, Matt. Helen, it's not safe for you to have one phone in this house. I mean it. It's not an extravagance to —

HELEN. They're coming Friday. I'll order another phone. Let's have some pizza.

JERRY. Pizza. Jesus. The thing is … (*Jerry takes a handkerchief out of his pocket and wipes his brow.*)

HELEN. Are you warm?

JERRY. A little.

HELEN. Why don't you take your coat off?

JERRY. I really can't stay.

HELEN. You could have a proper drink if you want. There's gin.

JERRY. No, thank you.

HELEN. One martini won't kill you.

JERRY. No, thank you. Matt, come on, get up. Give your mother back her chair. You're making me nervous in that thing. (*Matt wheels over to an arm chair.*) Look, I came over because there are a few things we should talk about. I thought maybe he and I would go to the city and talk about them and then later you and I would talk about stuff and then we would have all talked. That's what I was thinking. That was my plan. So why don't you get dressed, Matt? (*Matt has locked the chair and using the same technique as before, is attempting to get into the arm chair.*) What is he doing? What are you doing?

HELEN. Just sit down, Matt, would you.

MATT. I'm trying. (*Matt sits.*)

JERRY. I don't know what to do with you guys. (*To Matt.*) There's a lot going on right now. I need your help. Don't be playing games now, Matt, I mean it.

HELEN. I imagine it's not an easy time for you.

JERRY. No, it's not. You got my letter, right?

HELEN. Yes.

JERRY. Well, there's more. I don't know what he told you. She's been transferred. Sally. We have to move. Did he tell you this? I don't want to go, but I have to.

HELEN. Why are you going if you don't want to?

JERRY. I know it seems like California is far away and it is. But with planes, I can be back here in an afternoon. I mean, if there's an emergency I can come back.

HELEN. You hate flying.

JERRY. I'll get over it.

HELEN. You seem a little fraught. Why don't you have a proper drink?

JERRY. Fine. I'll have a proper drink. It's a good idea. We should all have a proper drink. *(Jerry goes to the kitchen. Helen stands up and walks over to get the remote control. They whisper …)*

MATT. What are you doing?

HELEN. I'm putting on Guy Lombardo.

MATT. He doesn't want to be here.

HELEN. *(Off the TV.)* Why isn't this working?

MATT. He's moving to California. Just let him go.

HELEN. What is wrong with this?

MATT. You unplugged it. *(Helen looks toward the kitchen and then gets up and rushes to plug the TV back in.)*

JERRY. *(Offstage.)* I can't find anything.

HELEN. *(Calling out.)* I'm sorry. The liquor is in the pantry now. Mrs. Green moved it, I forgot.

JERRY. *(Offstage.)* I got it. I got it. *(Jerry reenters with two bottles of liquor. Helen has just managed to sit in the wheelchair before Jerry notices her. He's a little confused how quickly she got in it.)* Do you want a whiskey sour? *(Jerry is looking at the couch.)*

HELEN. I would love a whiskey sour. *(Jerry moves to the cabinet to mix the drinks.)* So, who wants to watch Guy Lombardo?

MATT. He's not on yet.

HELEN. Okay. It was just an idea.

JERRY. Your car looks great out there. How does it run?

MATT. Are you asking me?

JERRY. No, I'm asking your mother.

HELEN. Well, obviously, I wouldn't know.

JERRY. I forgot the ice. *(Jerry goes into the kitchen. Helen rolls over to Matt. They whisper again.)*

HELEN. Stop behaving like an ass.

MATT. Me? You're acting like you're on a date. It's disgusting.

HELEN. Why don't you go to your room, if you're going to be like this?

MATT. Nothing would make me happier. Give me the chair.

HELEN. Here. Take it. *(Helen rolls the chair over to Matt.)*

MATT. Move it closer.

HELEN. I will.

MATT. Lock it.

HELEN. I know.

MATT. Hurry up.

HELEN. *(Angry.)* I hope you have a great New Year's Eve.

MATT. You too.

JERRY. *(Reentering with the ice.)* I filled the ice trays back up, just so you know. *(Matt's back in the wheelchair. Helen just makes it back onto the sofa before Jerry sees her. He is really confused now, but shakes it off and goes to the cabinet to continue mixing the drinks.)* I probably shouldn't be mixing champagne with gin, but what the hell. It's the holidays. Matt, you want a martini?

HELEN. Matt's going to lie down.

JERRY. I'm making him a martini.

MATT. *(To Helen.)* Can I have a martini?

HELEN. No. You can't.

JERRY. For Christ's sake, he can have a martini. We're all going to have a drink. It's a good idea. We have a lot of catching up to do and he's old enough to have a martini. *(Handing her a whiskey sour.)* Here. One whiskey sour.

HELEN. Thank you.

JERRY. Matt, come here. I'm going to show you how to do this. It's time you learned how to make a martini. A proper martini is made with Gin. Beefeater Gin. Vodka in a martini is not a martini. The trick is the Vermouth or more specifically, the lack of Vermouth. First of all you need a shaker.

HELEN. *(Off her whiskey sour.)* This is very good, honey.

JERRY. Thanks. Ideally, you should chill the Martini glass and the Vermouth. We don't have time for that. *(Demonstrating.)* But no matter what you swirl the Vermouth in the glass until the sides are coated and then you discard the remaining Vermouth. That's the important part. Discard it. Now spear a Spanish olive or two. We don't have any, but that's what you would normally do now and put it in the glass. Meanwhile pour the Gin in the shaker over copious amounts of ice. We don't have copious amounts of ice, but so be it. And don't shake it. You'll bruise it. That Bond guy's full of it. Stir it. If you shake it, you're going to water down the Gin. Maybe 007 likes his martinis weak, I don't. Then you strain it into a martini glass, which I'm glad to see you guys still have. *(Handing him the martini.)* Here. This isn't right, it's rushed. But at least you know now. You know how it's supposed to be done. *(Pouring his own martini.)* Technically, you're supposed to eat the olives first.

MATT. We don't have any olives.

JERRY. I know. But if we did. *(Picking up his martini.)* Cheers.

MATT. HELEN. Cheers. *(They drink.)*

JERRY. Do you like it?

MATT. Wow.

JERRY. Sip it.

HELEN. Remember when you taught him to ride a bike?

JERRY. I do, yes.

HELEN. This is so nice. All of us together. *(They drink some more.)* Do you remember when you taught him to play checkers?

JERRY. He beat me the next day.

HELEN. Let's get drunk tonight.

JERRY. Let's not and say we did.

HELEN. Well, I'm getting drunk.

JERRY. Knock yourself out. I've had enough this week. You know where I went last night?

HELEN. I wonder if the pizza's ready.

JERRY. Pete is still there.

HELEN. I put it in a half hour ago.

JERRY. Helen, I went to The Blue Canary last night. *(Beat.)* I haven't been there in years. *(Beat.)* The jukebox is still in the corner. *(Beat.)* Sorry. Maybe I shouldn't have brought it up.

MATT. You went to The Blue Canary last night?

JERRY. Helen, I didn't mean to upset you.

MATT. Did you meet anyone there?

JERRY. *(To Helen.)* I thought you'd be tickled.

MATT. Was there a woman there?

JERRY. What?

MATT. Was there a woman there?

JERRY. There are always woman at bars, Matt. That's why men go.

MATT. Did you talk to one?

JERRY. Excuse me?

MATT. Did you talk to one?

JERRY. Probably. I'm friendly.

MATT. Did she have blond hair?

HELEN. Stop it, Matt.

MATT. Tell me what you said to her?

JERRY. I didn't say anything.

MATT. You must have said something?

JERRY. I don't know what you're talking about.

MATT. Did you try and pick her up?

JERRY. You're totally out of line right now.

MATT. Did you dance with her?

JERRY. Who?

MATT. You shouldn't be trying to pick women up. They think you mean it.

HELEN. That's enough.

MATT. Oh, shut up.

JERRY. Don't tell your mother to shut up.

MATT. Somebody has to.

HELEN. Maybe he did mean it. Have you ever thought of that?

JERRY. I didn't try and pick anyone up.

MATT. I can't believe this.

JERRY. What is your problem? What is he talking about?

MATT. She knows what I'm talking about.

JERRY. Get up. Really. I've had it up to here with you. Get out of the chair.

MATT. Make her give me back the pen and I will.

HELEN. It's not his pen.

JERRY. Alright, stop it! I mean it! You two are like a bunch of crazy people. Do you know that? What am I supposed to do with you. Jesus. *(Silence.)* I have an idea. Let's all go see the ball drop. How about that? I'll take you both. I'm offering to take you both. We can all talk. I need to talk to you guys, okay? We can start the new year together. The three of us. Let me do something nice. It's a new decade. Let's try to look at the past in a good light. Can we just have some peace, please. The sixties are over. And not a minute too soon. Jesus. You know that ball's been dropping since 1908. Did you know that, Helen? That's amazing, isn't it? The ball first dropped in 1908. Sally heard that on the radio. She was driving around L.A. and heard that piece of trivia. Let's all go to Times Square. The three of us. Sally left on Wednesday. So it's just me. She would have stayed but she didn't want to get stuck here for too long. She couldn't do that. That's not good. Apparently it's not so good to fly, you know … The doctors don't recommend it. I guess the air pressure isn't the best thing in the world. Or maybe they're just afraid someone will go into labor at thirty thousand feet. I don't really know. I mean, she's only two months but, you know, she's a worrier. *(Beat.)* Hopefully no one will even notice at the wedding. *(Beat.)* I needed to tell you this personally. *(Jerry goes for more liquor. Beat.)*

MATT. Are you alright? *(Beat.)* Mom?

JERRY. That came out all wrong. You just make me crazy, both of you. I can't think straight. I want you to know that whatever happens, this is a family. We have a family. Change is good. It is. I mean, I don't know what the alternative is. Do you? We can't just be stuck in the past. It's New Year's Eve. I wanted to take you to see the ball drop. To listen to thousands of people cheer a new beginning. What do you want to do? Do you want to sit here and fight like we used to? Is that what you guys want? Do you want to watch the freaking ball drop on the freaking television set and eat frozen pizza. Is that what you want?

MATT. Mom, are you alright?

JERRY. God damn it! I don't love your mother anymore! She has to accept that. I have to accept it. We all do. *(Helen stands up. Jerry's looks right at her.)*

HELEN. Jerry.

JERRY. I'm not saying anything we don't already know. Don't look at me like that. *(Jerry faints.)*

MATT. Now what?

HELEN. I don't know.

MATT. Get some smelling salts.

HELEN. Smelling salts?

MATT. Splash some water on his face. *(Helen looks long and hard at Jerry.)*

HELEN. He's still in love with me.

MATT. No, he's not.

HELEN. Yes, he is. You weren't there. He asked me to go home with him.

MATT. He asked a blond woman in a bar.

HELEN. He never saw me. Why can't he see me? I'm standing. I'm standing. *(After a moment, Helen goes and gets a glass of water. She throws it in Jerry's face. Jerry starts to stir. Helen sits back down.)*

JERRY. Wow. Am I...? What time is it? Oh. I fell didn't I? *(He slowly gets up.)* I fainted. I'm alright. It's happened before. It's nothing. It's an anxiety attack. I'll be alright. These things are nothing. It's nerves. It's ... I'm hot. I never took my jacket off. *(He finds his drink.)* Really, it's purely psychological. Panic attacks. I swear I thought I saw you ... You don't want to know. It's all too much. Everything's too much right now. I'm fine. I'm fine. I think I want some club soda or something. Do you guys have any club soda?

MATT. No.

JERRY. Oh, well.

MATT. Why don't you go get some?

JERRY. That's alright. *(Beat.)* Should I?

MATT. Yeah.

JERRY. Do you need anything else?

MATT. No. Just get some soda.

JERRY. You don't need anything else?

MATT. No. *(Beat. Jerry leaves.)* Mom. *(Beat.)* Mom.

HELEN. What?

MATT. Do you smell that?

HELEN. What?

MATT. The pizza's burning.

HELEN. So what?

MATT. So, I want it. I'm hungry.

HELEN. It's awful. It's frozen like everything else.

MATT. It's not frozen anymore, it's probably in flames by now. Mom, turn off the oven. You can't let it burn.

HELEN. Why not? I hope the whole house burns down. I hope when your father comes back there's nothing left but insurance adjusters. *(Helen gets her coat and purse.)*

MATT. Where are you going?

HELEN. Out.

MATT. Give me the pen.

HELEN. Why should I?

MATT. Because I don't want to burn to a crisp, okay?

HELEN. He's making another family. Don't you care?

MATT. It's over now, Mom.

HELEN. I need more time.

MATT. No. It would never be enough.

HELEN. But you're going to leave me.

MATT. I'm supposed to leave you. I'm the only one in your life who's actually supposed to leave you.

HELEN. I never took a bath.

MATT. I'm sorry.

HELEN. But —

MATT. No. It's over. This is the way it is. We can't fix it. *(After a long moment, Helen goes to her purse and takes out the pen. She holds it.)*

HELEN. Will you do something for me?

MATT. What?

HELEN. Take my picture.

MATT. What did you do with the camera?

HELEN. It's over here. *(She goes to get the camera. Handing him the camera:)* Do you know how to use it?

MATT. Yeah. Hold on. I need to put the film in. *(Matt begins to load the film.)* That picture of you on Martha's Vineyard ... The one of you and Dad holding a beach ball ... I took it, didn't I?

HELEN. Yes.

MATT. Were you scared when it started?

HELEN. Terrified.

MATT. So was I.

HELEN. Where should I stand?

MATT. Over there.

HELEN. Where?

MATT. By the light.

HELEN. *(Moving to the light.)* I'm a little nervous.

MATT. So am I. My hands are shaking. *(Closing the camera.)* There. You ready? *(She takes her jacket off.)*

HELEN. Yes.

MATT. Smile. *(Pointing the camera.)* Say cheese. Mom, smile.

HELEN. *(Doing the best she can.)* I'm not good at that. I'm sorry.

MATT. *(Singing.)* "All I want for Christmas is my two front teeth ... "

HELEN. Stop it.

MATT. *(Singing.)* "All I want for Christmas is — "

HELEN. Alright, alright. *(Helen's smile widens.)*

MATT. There, that's better.

HELEN. How do I look?

MATT. You look beautiful. *(The flash goes off. Beat. Helen walks over and hands Matt the pen. He takes it and slowly stands up. They are both standing now. Helen ever so slightly stumbles.)* Wait. *(Silence. They stand there, looking at each other.)*

HELEN. You're taller than me.

MATT. I guess.

HELEN. The last time ... you only came up to my stomach. Look at you. You shave now, don't you?

MATT. Yeah.

HELEN. I wish it could have been like this. Both of us ...

MATT. Me too. *(Helen sits in the wheelchair.)*

HELEN. Turn off the oven. *(Matt goes to the kitchen, returning a few moments later.)* Is it burnt?

MATT. Pretty much.

HELEN. Go get the mail. I didn't look today.

MATT. It's a holiday.

HELEN. Tomorrow's the holiday. Go find out. Go. *(Matt puts his coat on over his pajamas. He puts his shoes on. He turns back to look at her before he leaves. Helen rolls over to the window and looks outside. Fade to black.)*

End of Play

PROPERTY LIST

Wheelchair
Lady's purse
Pens
TV remote control
3 wrapped presents: book and CD
College applications
Glass with alcoholic beverage
2 salads
Cocktail in glass
2 plates filled with food
Telephone
Blond wig
Several shopping bags of groceries
Sunglasses
Powder compact
Jacket or coat
Lady's wristwatch
A quarter
Jukebox
Glass of milk
Paper Towels
Bag of Oreos
High-heeled shoes
Ice bucket
2 bottles of champagne
3 champagne flutes
Man's cardigan sweater
2 bottles of liquor
Glass of water
Camera and film

SOUND EFFECTS

TV clips and commercials
Doorbell

NEW PLAYS

★ **THE EXONERATED by Jessica Blank and Erik Jensen.** Six interwoven stories paint a picture of an American criminal justice system gone horribly wrong and six brave souls who persevered to survive it. "The #1 play of the year...intense and deeply affecting..." *–NY Times.* "Riveting. Simple, honest storytelling that demands reflection." *–A.P.* "Artful and moving...pays tribute to the resilience of human hearts and minds." *–Variety.* "Stark...riveting...cunningly orchestrated." *–The New Yorker.* "Hard-hitting, powerful, and socially relevant." *–Hollywood Reporter.* [7M, 3W] ISBN: 0-8222-1946-8

★ **STRING FEVER by Jacquelyn Reingold.** Lily juggles the big issues: turning forty, artificial insemination and the elusive scientific Theory of Everything in this Off-Broadway comedy hit. "Applies the elusive rules of string theory to the conundrums of one woman's love life. Think *Sex and the City* meets *Copenhagen*." *–NY Times.* "A funny offbeat and touching look at relationships...an appealing romantic comedy populated by oddball characters." *–NY Daily News.* "Where kooky, zany, and madcap meet...whimsically winsome." *–NY Magazine.* "STRING FEVER will have audience members happily stringing along." *–TheaterMania.com.* "Reingold's language is surprising, inventive, and unique." *–nytheatre.com.* "...[a] whimsical comic voice." *–Time Out.* [3M, 3W (doubling)] ISBN: 0-8222-1952-2

★ **DEBBIE DOES DALLAS adapted by Erica Schmidt, composed by Andrew Sherman, conceived by Susan L. Schwartz.** A modern morality tale told as a comic musical of tragic proportions as the classic film is brought to the stage. "A scream! A saucy, tongue-in-cheek romp." *–The New Yorker.* "Hilarious! DEBBIE manages to have it all: beauty, brains and a great sense of humor!" *–Time Out.* "Shamelessly silly, shrewdly self-aware and proud of being naughty. Great fun!" *–NY Times.* "Racy and raucous, a lighthearted, fast-paced thoroughly engaging and hilarious send-up." *–NY Daily News.* [3M, 5W] ISBN: 0-8222-1955-7

★ **THE MYSTERY PLAYS by Roberto Aguirre-Sacasa.** Two interrelated one acts, loosely based on the tradition of the medieval mystery plays. "... stylish, spine-tingling...Mr. Aguirre-Sacasa uses standard tricks of horror stories, borrowing liberally from masters like Kafka, Lovecraft, Hitchcock...But his mastery of the genre is his own...irresistible." *–NY Times.* "Undaunted by the special-effects limitations of theatre, playwright and *Marvel* comic-book writer Roberto Aguirre-Sacasa maps out some creepy twilight zones in THE MYSTERY PLAYS, an engaging, related pair of one acts...The theatre may rarely deliver shocks equivalent to, say, *Dawn of the Dead*, but Aguirre-Sacasa's work is fine compensation." *–Time Out.* [4M, 2W] ISBN: 0-8222-2038-5

★ **THE JOURNALS OF MIHAIL SEBASTIAN by David Auburn.** This epic one-man play spans eight tumultuous years and opens a uniquely personal window on the Romanian Holocaust and the Second World War. "Powerful." *–NY Times.* "[THE JOURNALS OF MIHAIL SEBASTIAN] allows us to glimpse the idiosyncratic effects of that awful history on one intelligent, pragmatic, recognizably real man..." *–NY Newsday.* [3M, 5W] ISBN: 0-8222-2006-7

★ **LIVING OUT by Lisa Loomer.** The story of the complicated relationship between a Salvadoran nanny and the Anglo lawyer she works for. "A stellar new play. Searingly funny." *–The New Yorker.* "Both generous and merciless, equally enjoyable and disturbing." *–NY Newsday.* "A bitingly funny new comedy. The plight of working mothers is explored from two pointedly contrasting perspectives in this sympathetic, sensitive new play." *–Variety.* [2M, 6W] ISBN: 0-8222-1994-8

DRAMATISTS PLAY SERVICE, INC.
440 Park Avenue South, New York, NY 10016 212-683-8960 Fax 212-213-1539
postmaster@dramatists.com   www.dramatists.com

NEW PLAYS

★ **MATCH by Stephen Belber.** Mike and Lisa Davis interview a dancer and choreographer about his life, but it is soon evident that their agenda will either ruin or inspire them—and definitely change their lives forever. "Prolific laughs and ear-to-ear smiles." *–NY Magazine.* "Uproariously funny, deeply moving, enthralling theater. Stephen Belber's MATCH has great beauty and tenderness, and abounds in wit." *–NY Daily News.* "Three and a half out of four stars." *–USA Today.* "A theatrical steeplechase that leads straight from outrageous bitchery to unadorned, heartfelt emotion." *–Wall Street Journal.* [2M, 1W] ISBN: 0-8222-2020-2

★ **HANK WILLIAMS: LOST HIGHWAY by Randal Myler and Mark Harelik.** The story of the beloved and volatile country-music legend Hank Williams, featuring twenty-five of his most unforgettable songs. "[LOST HIGHWAY has] the exhilarating feeling of Williams on stage in a particular place on a particular night…serves up classic country with the edges raw and the energy hot…By the end of the play, you've traveled on a profound emotional journey: LOST HIGHWAY transports its audience and communicates the inspiring message of the beauty and richness of Williams' songs…forceful, clear-eyed, moving, impressive." *–Rolling Stone.* "…honors a very particular musical talent with care and energy… smart, sweet, poignant." *–NY Times.* [7M, 3W] ISBN: 0-8222-1985-9

★ **THE STORY by Tracey Scott Wilson.** An ambitious black newspaper reporter goes against her editor to investigate a murder and finds the *best* story…but at what cost? "A singular new voice…deeply emotional, deeply intellectual, and deeply musical…" *–The New Yorker.* "…a conscientious and absorbing new drama…" *–NY Times.* "… a riveting, tough-minded drama about race, reporting and the truth…" *–A.P.* "… a stylish, attention-holding script that ends on a chilling note that will leave viewers with much to talk about." *–Curtain Up.* [2M, 7W (doubling, flexible casting)] ISBN: 0-8222-1998-0

★ **OUR LADY OF 121st STREET by Stephen Adly Guirgis.** The body of Sister Rose, beloved Harlem nun, has been stolen, reuniting a group of life-challenged childhood friends who square off as they wait for her return. "A scorching and dark new comedy… Mr. Guirgis has one of the finest imaginations for dialogue to come along in years." *–NY Times.* "Stephen Guirgis may be the best playwright in America under forty." *–NY Magazine.* [8M, 4W] ISBN: 0-8222-1965-4

★ **HOLLYWOOD ARMS by Carrie Hamilton and Carol Burnett.** The coming-of-age story of a dreamer who manages to escape her bleak life and follow her romantic ambitions to stardom. Based on Carol Burnett's bestselling autobiography, *One More Time.* "…pure theatre and pure entertainment…" *–Talkin' Broadway.* "…a warm, fuzzy evening of theatre." *–BrodwayBeat.com.* "…chuckles and smiles of recognition or surprise flow naturally…a remarkable slice of life." *–TheatreScene.net.* [5M, 5W, 1 girl] ISBN: 0-8222-1959-X

★ **INVENTING VAN GOGH by Steven Dietz.** A haunting and hallucinatory drama about the making of art, the obsession to create and the fine line that separates truth from myth. "Like a van Gogh painting, Dietz's story is a gorgeous example of excess—one that remakes reality with broad, well-chosen brush strokes. At evening's end, we're left with the author's resounding opinions on art and artifice, and provoked by his constant query into which is greater: van Gogh's art or his violent myth." *–Phoenix New Times.* "Dietz's writing is never simple. It is always brilliant. Shaded, compressed, direct, lucid—he frames his subject with a remarkable understanding of painting as a physical experience." *–Tucson Citizen.* [4M, 1W] ISBN: 0-8222-1954-9

DRAMATISTS PLAY SERVICE, INC.
440 Park Avenue South, New York, NY 10016 212-683-8960 Fax 212-213-1539
postmaster@dramatists.com www.dramatists.com

NEW PLAYS

★ **INTIMATE APPAREL by Lynn Nottage.** The moving and lyrical story of a turn-of-the-century black seamstress whose gifted hands and sewing machine are the tools she uses to fashion her dreams from the whole cloth of her life's experiences. "...Nottage's play has a delicacy and eloquence that seem absolutely right for the time she is depicting..." *–NY Daily News.* "...thoughtful, affecting...The play offers poignant commentary on an era when the cut and color of one's dress—and of course, skin—determined whom one could and could not marry, sleep with, even talk to in public." *–Variety.* [2M, 4W] ISBN: 0-8222-2009-1

★ **BROOKLYN BOY by Donald Margulies.** A witty and insightful look at what happens to a writer when his novel hits the bestseller list. "The characters are beautifully drawn, the dialogue sparkles..." *–nytheatre.com.* "Few playwrights have the mastery to smartly investigate so much through a laugh-out-loud comedy that combines the vintage subject matter of successful writer-returning-to-ethnic-roots with the familiar mid-life crisis." *–Show Business Weekly.* [4M, 3W] ISBN: 0-8222-2074-1

★ **CROWNS by Regina Taylor.** Hats become a springboard for an exploration of black history and identity in this celebratory musical play. "Taylor pulls off a Hat Trick: She scores thrice, turning CROWNS into an artful amalgamation of oral history, fashion show, and musical theater..." *–TheatreMania.com.* "...wholly theatrical...Ms. Taylor has created a show that seems to arise out of spontaneous combustion, as if a bevy of department-store customers simultaneously decided to stage a revival meeting in the changing room." *–NY Times.* [1M, 6W (2 musicians)] ISBN: 0-8222-1963-8

★ **EXITS AND ENTRANCES by Athol Fugard.** The story of a relationship between a young playwright on the threshold of his career and an aging actor who has reached the end of his. "[Fugard] can say more with a single line than most playwrights convey in an entire script...Paraphrasing the title, it's safe to say this drama, making its memorable entrance into our consciousness, is unlikely to exit as long as a theater exists for exceptional work." *–Variety.* "A thought-provoking, elegant and engrossing new play..." *–Hollywood Reporter.* [2M] ISBN: 0-8222-2041-5

★ **BUG by Tracy Letts.** A thriller featuring a pair of star-crossed lovers in an Oklahoma City motel facing a bug invasion, paranoia, conspiracy theories and twisted psychological motives. "...obscenely exciting...top-flight craftsmanship. Buckle up and brace yourself..." *–NY Times.* "...[a] thoroughly outrageous and thoroughly entertaining play...the possibility of enemies, real and imagined, to squash has never been more theatrical." *–A.P.* [3M, 2W] ISBN: 0-8222-2016-4

★ **THOM PAIN (BASED ON NOTHING) by Will Eno.** An ordinary man muses on childhood, yearning, disappointment and loss, as he draws the audience into his last-ditch plea for empathy and enlightenment. "It's one of those treasured nights in the theater—treasured nights anywhere, for that matter—that can leave you both breathless with exhilaration and...in a puddle of tears." *–NY Times.* "Eno's words...are familiar, but proffered in a way that is constantly contradictory to our expectations. Beckett is certainly among his literary ancestors." *–nytheatre.com.* [1M] ISBN: 0-8222-2076-8

★ **THE LONG CHRISTMAS RIDE HOME by Paula Vogel.** Past, present and future collide on a snowy Christmas Eve for a troubled family of five. "...[a] lovely and hauntingly original family drama...a work that breathes so much life into the theater." *–Time Out.* "...[a] delicate visual feast..." *–NY Times.* "...brutal and lovely...the overall effect is magical." *–NY Newsday.* [3M, 3W] ISBN: 0-8222-2003-2

DRAMATISTS PLAY SERVICE, INC.
440 Park Avenue South, New York, NY 10016 212-683-8960 Fax 212-213-1539
postmaster@dramatists.com   www.dramatists.com